The Model
and its
Architecture

The Model and its Architecture

Patrick Healy

010 Publishers **Rotterdam 2008**

In their publication of 1974, *Inleiding tot het modelbegrip*, Kees Bertels and Doede Nauta provided an account of the concept of model which displayed, and continues to do so, some of the difficulties of defining and approaching that concept. Some of the definitions current at the time of their writing were themselves exemplary of the complexity of, and differences within, the concept of the model.[1] The notion of model could mean an actual physical model, that is, an artefact such that its parts, their relations and its working are suitably analogous to some other system. There was also the idea of a purely conceptual model, or what was called a 'merely' conceptual model, which was the envisaging or the specification in words of an artefact as described, without actually building it. Thus a verbal description of an actual physical model could be called a conceptual model. This could also imply that there was an envisaging or specification in words of a system simpler in various ways than some other system of which it is the model; simpler but not otherwise dissimilar, and further, the tendency to call any theory whatsoever a model, insofar as any theory tends to possess, at least unwittingly, the features intended to characterise models in the simple specification of words functioning as a conceptual model.

For the economist Schumpeter, model building was nothing other than the conscious attempt at systematisation of concepts and relations.[2] The logician Tarski restricts the definition to the possible realisation in which all valid sentences of a theory T are satisfied, and this is called a model of T.[3]

Ackoff points to some of the complex linguistic usage of the term: 'the word model is used as a noun, adjective, and verb, and in each instance it has a slightly different connotation'.[4] As a noun 'model' is a representation in the sense in which an architect constructs a small-scale model of a building or a physicist a large-scale model of an atom. As an adjective 'model' implies a degree of perfection or idealisation, as in reference to a model home, or a model husband. As a verb 'to model' means to demonstrate, to reveal, to show what a thing is like.

Scientific models have all these connotations. They are representations of objects, states, events. They are idealised in the sense that they are less complicated than reality and hence easier to use for research purposes. From the latter point Ackoff suggests that models are easier to manipulate than the real thing, and that there is a process of abstraction in which only the relevant properties of reality are represented. This echoes the view of the material model in science as a representation of a complex system which is assumed simpler and also to have properties similar to those selected for study in the original complex system.

Perrin has recently shown that the work of Hertz, and his publication *Die Prinzipien der Mechanik in neuem Zusammenhang dargestellt*, published in Leipzig in 1894, provided an account

1 Kees Bertels and Doede Nauta, **Inleiding tot het Modelbegrip** (Amsterdam: Wetenschappelijke Uitgeverij BV, 1974).
2 This can be found in: J.A. Schumpeter, **History of Economic Analysis** (Oxford University Press, 1954), p.562. Model building: conscious attempts at systematisation of concepts and relations.
3 For discussion of this, see: Doede Nauta, **Logica en Model** (Hilversum: De Haan, 1969). Tarski's definition comes from his **Undecidable Theories** (Amsterdam: North Holland Publishing, 1953), p.11.
4 Russell L. Ackoff, **Scientific Method** (New York: Wiley, 1962), p.108; and his 'On the Use of Models in Corporate Planning', in **Strategic Management Journal**, vol.2, 1981, pp.353-359.

of the model and image which is significant for Wittgenstein.[5] Hertz suggests we form internal simulacra – *innere Scheinbilder* – of external objects in such a way that the necessary theoretical consequences of images – *Bilder* – are always images of the necessary and real consequences of the objects represented – *abgebildeten*. Images permit, on his account, the ability to anticipate future experiences in a way that allows us to organise our current state on the basis of such anticipations. Images are proleptic.

Hertz defines his concept of image-model in the following terms: a mechanical system is called a dynamic model (*Modell*) if the connections can be represented by co-ordinates which satisfy the following conditions: 1) the number of co-ordinates of the first is equal to the number of the other; 2) that if one establishes an appropriate correlation (*Zuordnung*) between the co-ordinates, the same condition equations are valid for both systems; 3) the measures of displacement in the systems coincide when one adopts this correlation. What is of further interest is that this is close to the idea of image in the *Tractatus* of Wittgenstein, in that the image is a model of what it depicts, and which requires the same multiplicity as that which it shows. The essential point is not the question of resemblance, but what in mathematical terms is referred to as isomorphism, which binds the image and the fact, and what is equally significant is that the essential is not to copy this, but to model it. Thought then can be a method of projection which utilises the proposition, and in Hertz's conception thoughts are also a dynamic model of reality; even if thought is without colour, sound or spatiality, it still depicts the state of affairs.

Some of the wider implications of the role of models and analogies in science have been studied by Giuseppe Del Re.[6] He argues that models fall into two categories, which he calls the mathematical/physical model. The mathematical model is an essential tool for the cognition of things not directly accessible to the senses. Physical models are objects which belong to the world directly accessible to direct experience. They are often constructed *ad hoc* and possibly idealised; they serve as referents for analogies, which appear to be indispensable in most aspects of scientific theorising, especially for the submicroscopic levels of reality. In that sense they provide an argument for structure and shape as characteristic molecular properties. Indeed, Del Re accepts the claim that a sapient use of models is the essential trait of Galilean science, in this sense that models are then taken as tools of scientific thinking, performing often the role of *Gedankenexperimente*. Physical models are tools of descriptive analogical functional thinking, whereas mathematical models, in the main, are the tools of argumentative, analogical thinking.

Del Re wants to enquire as to the way in which physical models provide images. Science selects patterns of events and treats them as identical real entities that differ only by accidental details. For example, Del Re points out that the statement that ammonia and hydrochloric acid react to give ammonium chloride is true when one understands that it is subject to three limitations: first, that it refers to pure substance; second, there is no introduction of time evolution or process, and third, it does not describe details of actual experiment. From this he concludes that the physical world of science is not the real world. Science works with a world of 'shadow types', a copy of the world of sensible experience in which only standard objects (types) are admitted. He concludes that one meaning of 'model' in science is an appeal to shadow types under consideration. In that sense Max Weber's 'ideal types' could also be considered as effective scientific models.[7]

The second aspect of the image provided is that it stabilises and uses analogy to indicate what is under inspection. In the size-ladder notion of the physical world – that is, a world which extends from intergalactic gas cloud to planets such as Mars; the Pacific Ocean; the Himalayas; an ecosystem; the Schwarzwald; a whale; an oak tree; a human being; a bee; a microscopic mite; DNA molecules; hydrogen atoms; photons, and a neutron – the issue of direct access to reality seems to extend from infinity to infinity.

A molecule cannot even be seen by simple magnification, because it is smaller than the wavelength of visible light; so what we call an image obtained by scanning tunnel microscopy is a theoretical construction based on formal similarity between matter and light waves. Each object belongs to one size-level, whereas different complexity levels are present in any given object. Del Re makes then the observation that knowledge based on analogies with *ad hoc* objects – possibly artificial as in the string-ball model of molecules – indicates how important analogies are, in that they enable the expression of abstract concepts and processes.

In the interrelation between real size, direct access, and the physical model belonging to the direct access level, one, for example, assumes that atoms exist, which are visualised as tiny spheres, and the elements are then assumed to be made of identical atoms; pure substance is then defined in terms of elements, molecules are assumed to be groups of atoms and visualised as a cluster of spheres and so on and so forth. In his consideration of the materiality of molecular modelling, Eric Francoeur has further suggested that the practise of physical molecular modelling is rather simple.

What molecular modelling involves is the production and use of three-dimensional structures that render, more or less to scale, the spatial position of atoms (or groups of atoms) in a molecular structure, as well as the bonds between them. Most molecular models are assembled from commercially available modelling kits, which has led to the proliferation of conventions and tools. There has been, in Francoeur's view, a move from representation in scientific practice, to representation *as* scientific practice.[8]

---

5 This information can be followed in: Denis Perrin, 'Wittgenstein et le clair-obscur de l'image', in **L'image**, ed. Alexander Schnell (Paris: Vrin, 2007), pp.91-113.

6 Giuseppe Del Re, 'Models and Analysis in Science', in **Hyle, International Journal for Philosophy of Chemistry**, vol.6, 2000, no.1, pp.5-15.

7 For this argument see: Jürgen Ritsert, **Models and Concepts of Ideology** (Amsterdam: Rodopi, 1990), chapter four: 'Action, Interest and Reflection – Weber and Weberian Models of Scientific Knowledge', pp.70-103.

8 Eric Francoeur, 'The Forgotten Tool: The Design and Use of Molecular Models', in **Social Studies of Science**, 27, 1997, pp.7-40. Also see: Pierre Laszlo, 'Playing with Molecular Models', in **Hyle**, vol.6, 2000, no.1, pp.85-97. A special issue of **Hyle** devoted to chemistry and model-making.

His view suggests that there is indeed a passage from things in themselves, or the semiological realm of raw materiality, to graphematic space. This passage constitutes the powerful functionality of inscription. Francoeur looks at the translation not through further graphematics, but as translation into synthetic objects, or structural models. Physical and graphical representation in the laboratory is equally eidetic. This point is reinforced by a distinction once made by Galison in his work *Images and Logic*, and applied by Francoeur, namely that any representation of molecular structure does not stand in homomorphic relation to a referent 'out-there', but only to other structural representations.[9] They therefore should be considered as 'synthetic' representations, or interpretations that stand in a homologic relation to empirical events and experimental phenomena which they can be construed as explaining or predicting.

The stronger argument that emerges is that there can be no such thing as comparing structural representation of a molecule to the 'real thing', since it is through representational work that a molecular structure becomes coherently visible. Francoeur then adds that the realm of molecular structures is essentially cultural, co-extensive with the means chemists have given themselves to show, talk about, and work with structures, means which are *ceteris paribus* epistemically equivalent while phenomenologically distinct.

Here one also sees the long consequence of Nietzsche's consideration in his seminal 'Über Warheit und Lüge im Aussermoralischen Sinn', itself a complex fable that clever animals of the planet invented knowledge and took their intellect and intellectual activity to be the centre of the world.[10]

Of their number, the most proud are the philosophers who think that the world turns on their thoughts and actions. In this distortion lies a monstrous claim which ignores that our intellect is is simply another means of survival in the struggle for existence. The main way intellect shows itself is in pretending; the weak use feigning and deception, dissimulation, when confronted by the stronger. Mankind is the highest exhibition of the ability to deceive and simulate. But no individual can manage this alone, and in order to survive the dependency on others makes a truce in the struggle necessary, a fictional treaty which results in peace for a while.

It is this fiction which is the origin of truth and the source of the contrast between the truth and the lie. Thus even language is a result of conventions, which produces signs to denote objects. Language is not the result of knowledge of things, and denotations do not form a 'fit' for the facts. Thus there is no correspondence theory of truth.

---

9 Peter Galison, **Images and Logic: A Material Culture of Microphysics** (Chicago: University of Chicago Press, 1997).
10 Friedrich Nietzsche, **Sämtliche Werke**, Vol.I, eds. Colli and Montinari (Berlin: De Gruyter, 1980), pp. 873-91.

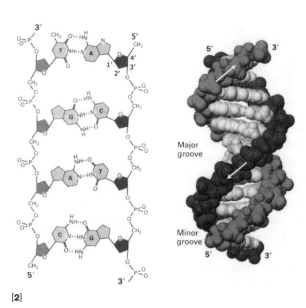

[1]

[2]

[4]

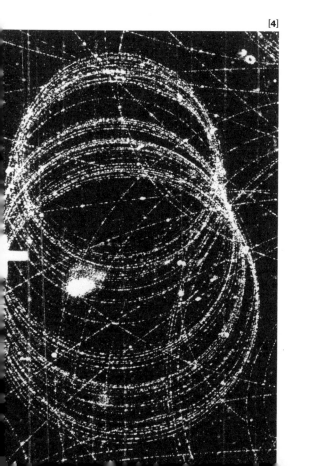

[3]

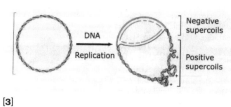

1 The domus chymisi (house of chemistry) in Libavius's **Alchymia**.
2 The structure of double-stranded DNA.
3 DNA replication introduces DNA supercoiling.
4 Cloud chamber atlas.

[1]

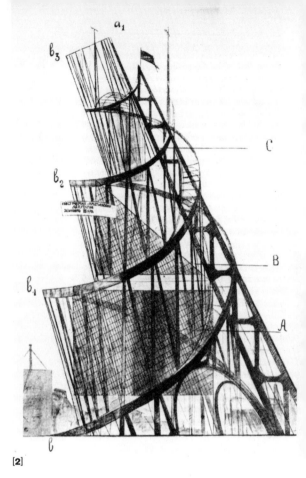

[2]

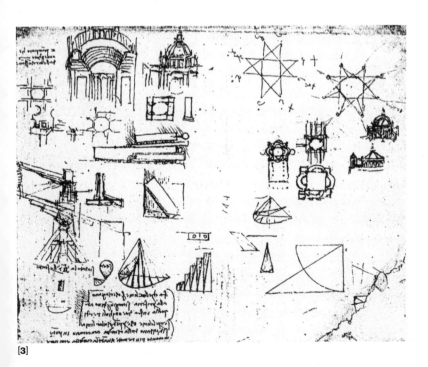

[3]

1 B.M. Iofan and I.V. Zholtovsky, Palace of the Soviets, second project, 1934.
2 Vladimir Tatlin, Monument to the Third International.
3 Leonardo da Vinci, Codex Atlanticus, f 271 v-d.

Nietzsche says that this point is obvious if we examine the variety and means by which many different languages draw distinctions and demarcations in an arbitrary way. Thus we have to understand 'metaphor' and 'concept'. We rely on metaphors of things to advance a claim to know things in themselves, and these metaphors are far from any correspondence to original entities. Where words are transformed into concepts, this already means that we abandon the singular, completely individualised original experience, the *Urerlebnis* which gives rise to it, and trade in experience as generalised comparison. A concept is never a complete fit for an individual case.

The concept arises by identifying the non-identical. The example of the leaf is given by Nietzsche, in that no individual leaf is identical with any other, and the concept of leaf arose out of an arbitrary process of cancelling individual differences.

Jürgen Ritsert makes the point that Nietzsche has not really left the problem of what he calls Fichte's circle. These are the compelling words of Fichte that Ritsert cites in his account of the problem in *Models and the Concepts of Ideology*:

This, that finite mind necessarily has to posit something absolutely outside of himself (a thing in itself) and yet has to acknowledge, on the other hand, that it exists only for him (being a necessary *noumenon*) and represents that circle which he has to expand into infinity, but out of which he cannot step.
From Fichte's *Grundlage der gesamten Wissenschaftslehre*, 1794.

It is the oblivion to differences that allows the myth of concepts as ideas which grasp essence or the true nature of things in themselves. There are in nature no forms and concepts, and Nietzsche will add, no natural kinds, rather only what is inaccessible and indefinable for us. Nietzsche then deploys a metaphor to talk about 'truth', which is an agile and flexible army of metaphors, metonymies, and anthropomorphisms, used so often by some tribe they appear inevitable, and being truthful only really means that we keep to our customary metaphors.

The 'lie' that is obliged in this is, and I follow Ritsert's interpretation here, that our concepts have to miss the unrepresentable singularity of events. We speak according to convention, we lie out of fidelity to the tribe and its linguistic conventions. Otherwise we are excluded and treated as outsiders. In Nietzsche's scenario, 'reasonable persons' submit themselves to the 'dominion of abstractions'.

The immediacy of the moment is lost, betrayed in some higher instance; metaphors that are vivid and striking are reduced to schemes, images with fatidic and fatal power are transformed into concepts. Thus the emergence of hierarchy, casts and grades.

The singular and incomparable event of the particular image and metaphor is forced into the 'roman columbarium' of conceptual order which claims to supply something more firm, general, better known and more human. The fullest development of Nietzsche's think-ing, as indicated below, is to be found in Deleuze's primary text *Difference and Repetition.*

For Nietzsche the sclerosis of metaphor drains the vitality of experience, and hardens and stiffens the 'mass of images' which flow from the original faculty of human phantasy. Truth claims, or validity claims – *Geltungsanspruch* – are nothing more than the constraint exercised by the 'dominion of abstractions'. Powers of abstraction which dominate discourse turn discourse into the tomb of impressions.

Nietzsche posits a tense disjunction between the 'reasonable man' and 'intuitive man'. However, neither can dispense with the fundamental exigency of dissimu-lation and artifice, which belongs to any symbolic practice. Ritsert makes the point that reasonable or rational man has to pay the price by constantly working on the affirmation of discourse, permanently establishing its regulating forces and its constraints on the course of the individual life, and therefore, uninten-tionally, supports its imaginary (ideological) qualities which consist in the 'lie', the regime of abstraction over intuition.[11]

Intuitive man aims at the dominion of life by art, and even in the drive to tear the web of delusion apart, cannot avoid the imaginary quality of any sym-bolic practice. The 'lie' is necessary for existence, even during the conduct of the truce, in the struggle for survival, and human life transformed into beauty and appearance by the intuitive type, posited as the real, is also a form of drastic obliteration.

How all these relations cohere is by the force of ideology, which also consti-tutes the subject within the imaginary loop. This is the reality of representation, not the act of *Wiederspiegelung*, of an isometric mirroring, which is then some-how falsified or distorted. The imaginary becomes, through re-presentation, over and over, presented to individuals in their real existence, as the power of relations itself. So it is not that existing relations of production are represented, but what is re-presented, is the polarity where there is a subject, and real conditions of existence. This is what allows the functioning of actors in the social whole.

Althusser's working of Nietzsche's situation is caught well in his famous def-inition of ideology: 'L'idéologie interpelle les individus en sujets'.[12] The paradox is that to make people compliant, an illusion of freedom and liberty, an imagin-ary, symbolic order must be first introduced as 'subject'. This is not the idea of the 'other' through recognition constructing the subject; rather, it is the more complex way in which meaning-systems, and imaginary relations, are mobilised into significations, which cannot be then reduced either to something repre-sented, nor to a source in the acting subject, as they simply are the effects of the means of representation in which the ultimate aim is the submission to the hegemonical signification. However, no matter what the complex instauration of ideological and imaginary processes is for the construction of the real, it is still the supposition that 3D models are seen as more real than their graphic counterparts. This can be seen in the claim of Ferguson, in his *Engineering and the Mind's Eye*, that the advantages of models is that they take the observer one step closer to reality than can a drawing.[13]

The notion of reality for Ferguson is more phenomenological than epistemic, as shown in his argument: when the observer wants to see around the corner of an object in a perspective drawing, he or she is convinced that there lies the missing piece of the puzzle of understanding. A model permits the observer not merely to look around the corner, but Ferguson says, it lets one walk around it, look down on and up at the object, and allows one to receive tactile clues that help make sense of the object.

Models then are an embodiment that frees the viewer from the constraint of perspective in that they do not impose a single point of view, they allow things to be held as constant, and they can be manifested to investigate and explore articulation of their components, they introduce a haptic dimension, and they introduce a hybrid phenomenological realm, what could be termed a post-inscriptive realm. Such a realm transcends the dichotomy between things and inscriptions and seeks to capitalise on the functionality of the pre-inscriptive material world, where functionalities are perceived as an asset rather than a liability.

In modelling of the environmental, taken as complex natural systems, it can be seen that the number of different non-equivalent descriptions of a system has been equated with the complexity of the system. One also sees that there are different concepts of complexity at work, descriptive, complex non-linear dynamical systems, and out of this an emerging model which can be called the complexity model. It has been suggested that dynamical systems have become the formal model in the discovery of complexity across a range of disciplines, and thus ecosystems modelled and simulated as if they were dynamical systems. In a sense the model developed becomes itself complex and displays the use and interaction between three different kinds of model. Firstly, there are behavioural or descriptive models, which include functional, empirical 'black-box' models, or what is called 'utilization' technology in forestry, agriculture or water management. The latter of course is the direct source for the development of the 'Polder Model'. One finds a second class in the elementary structure models used to elucidate and determine basic processes. Finally, there are the 'real structure' models, that make use of supposedly 'real' empirical parameters.[14]

Even in the conflation of these three models, there is an understanding that scientific models are largely heuristic and, as Kretzenbacher has argued in his article 'The Aesthetics and Heuristics of Analogy', their role of simulating bi-geo-chemical processes in ecosystems should often be treated as learning instruments that provide a catalyst for interdisciplinary communication.[15] There is still a large element of tinkering and bricolage in these processes.

11 See note 7.

12 Louis Althusser, **Positions** (Paris, 1976). For a fuller discussion, see: Saül Karsz, **Théorie et politique: Louis Althusser** (Paris: Fayard, 1974).

13 Eugene Ferguson, **Engineering and the Mind's Eye** (Cambridge, MA: MIT Press, 1992), p.107.

14 System metaphors pervade ecology and the environmental sciences. Ecosystems have been treated, modelled and simulated as if they were dynamical systems. Dynamic systems has become the formal paradigm across a range of disciplines, introducing the discovery of complexity, as descriptive, ontological, dynamical and emergent.

15 Leopold Kretzenbacher, 'The Aesthetics and Heuristics of Analogy: Model and Metaphor in Chemical Communication', in **Hyle**, 9-2, 2003, pp.191-218.

[1]

[2]

[3]

1 G. Bruyns, design model of MSc thesis
work entitled **Post-Colonial-Urban-
Tribe-Space**, Delft University of Technology,
2002. Photo: G. Bruyns.
2 Receding Glacial Maximums, Antarctica.
3 Part of map of Ouderkerk Polder,
Netherlands, 1899.

[1]

[2]

[3]

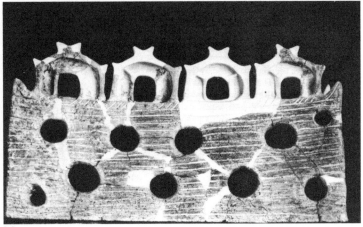

[4]

1 Stonehenge, Salisbury (England),
c. 2750-1500 BC.
2 Clay model of sanctuary with hole on top
for inserting goddess.
3 Clay model of sanctuary consisting of two
temples supported on a substructure and
topped by a ram's and a bull's head.
4 Clay model of an edifice from Cscioarele,
lower Danube region, showing a large
substructure supporting four temples.

Objects could exist which function as models but are not usually so considered by name. Thus a model could be the concrete representation of a situation or entities, events, from nature or history mediated through a symbolic gathering. Berthel and Nauta point to the existence of a small-scale house, which may or may not function as a model, and to the example of Stonehenge which, following then recent discussion, they suggest can be viewed as an earth-bound observatory which modelled in the placement of the stones important astronomical alignements, which could then be viewed as a model in stone of the heavenly circuits.[16] Current research explores the therapeutic significance of Stonehenge, and as a pilgrim place for healing. This example points to one of the chief difficulties of tracing historical accounts of the model itself. A notorious and difficult thesis on *The Gods and Goddesses of Old Europe* is strewn with objects which are referred to as 'model of', and which may just be *post factum* miniatures or replicas, etc.[17] This problem has been noted in Sardo's *La Figurazione Plastica dell'Architettura*, and his treatment of the conception of the model for early historical periods is subsequently very summary in its execution.[18]

The examination of the word model and its etymology also points to the 'noun, adjective, verb' problem of the usage noted above by Ackoff. The original form of the word is Latin as *modulus*, with the primary meaning of small-scale, scale. This is the way the term is used in the first century before the common era. It can be localised in the writing of Vitruvius. The rediscovery of the text of Vitruvius gave obvious impetus to the usage of the term in the early Renaissance, and the word shifts from *modulus* to *modellus*, and a further connotation of 'form' was also implied. In middle-High German the word *modell* is clearly a loanword from the Latin, probably imported from lodges of builders in the South of France, or brought directly to Germany by itinerant craftsmen coming from France during the 8th century. In the French language usage the term also moves towards the idea of *modulus = molde*, which comes into English as 'mould'.[19]

The explosion of studies concerned with the model and modelling in science also has further intensified what one scholar has called the 'muddle of the model'. The contemporary set of problematics in determining a paradigm was initiated by Thomas Kuhn's powerful and adversial text *The Structure of Scientific Revolution*.[20]

Kuhn's text rapidly established itself as one of the most significant in the philosophy of science after the war, and remains a touchstone for understanding how the difference between normal and revolutionary science works. Much of its argument hinges on the concept of paradigm itself, and it is often the case that in his text the meaning of paradigm subtly interchanges with that of model.

Kuhn's arguments are of some complexity; as he needs to distinguish revolutionary from

---

16 Their view on Stonehenge was taken from G.S. Hawkins, **Stonehenge Decoded** (New York: Doubleday, 1966).
17 Marija Gimbutas, **The Goddesses and Gods of Old Europe** (London: Thames and Hudson, reprint, 2007).
18 Nicolò Sardo, **La Figurazione plastica dell'architettura** (Rome: Edizioni Kappa, 2004).
19 See note 1, pp.33-40, for an overview of linguistic evidence.
20 For a fuller discussion, see my **Images of Knowledge** (Amsterdam: Sun, 2005).

normal, he also deploys the working of the paradigm as being shifted through a particular historical epoch, thus the meaning of paradigm after Newton is not the same as before. Further he requires a reading of paradigm which also remains open-ended and which allows for the emergence of anomaly and novelty, what becomes itself part of the new understanding of paradigm. Kuhn's main aim is to shift the 'image of science of which we are possessed'. He draws on historical studies to accomplish this, without providing an account of how the historical itself had become scientific, nor indeed whether such a procedure could without an account of what had substantially changed, be accepted as valid. In other words, Kuhn cannot ground the procedures by which he identifies processes.

Part of the difficulty is his manner of identifying the paradigm, both as exemplar and pattern, and at the same time as the probative model for an agreed and consensual understanding of a scientific community. The actual proliferation of the sciences and specialisations makes the idea of a community less and less understandable. The problem of defining for example the way in which even text books could function as models in pre-17th century science and the examples drawn from the arguments about electricity, or the claim that says that the work of Newton shifts the nature of the exemplary, while themselves exemplifying ruptures with regard to earlier periods, make it difficult to interpret the Kuhnian paradigm, which he proposes as anything other than a highly circular activity.

Throughout Kuhn's text there are semantic slippages which subtly move the early concept of paradigm to eventually something like 'family resemblance'. This involves more than just a performative contradiction. The circumstances which made the shift of paradigm possible for science, are themselves the core claim of any rational account, and to abandon them is effectively to abandon the very procedure which would make such an analysis possible, or warranted. The criticism of Kuhn in no way diminishes the significance of his work, and one of the counter claims for his version of research in paradigm is that this has effectively usurped previous theories and has itself dominated the field. It might be too harsh to suggest that such a defence is a version of 'might is right', or to follow Steve Fuller's very politicised reading of what he takes to be the highly conservative agenda of Kuhn's work.[21]

It can be argued that the study of the shift in paradigms drew attention to the problem of model building. However, one can see in the turn of philosophical investigation in the work of Deleuze specifically a turn to the concrete, and a real philosophical determination to seek a new image of thought.

With the writing of the Deleuze text *Difference and Repetition*, the anti-Platonism of what Deleuze named a purer empiricism was also announced, with immediate and even devastating consequences for the tradition of aesthetic reflection inherited from Kant and Hegel. Deleuze sets out the long consequences of what he sees as the central philosophical inheritance of the model, and affirms against its ontological priority a philosophy of simulacrum.

Deleuze described *Difference and Repetition* as the first book in which he was to 'do philosophy', and claimed that all his books, even the ones with Guattari, are connected to this work. What he sought in concentrating on the problem of difference and repetition was how to arrive at a concept of difference without subordinating it to the Same, Similar, Opposed or to the Analogous.[22] Deleuze refers to his project as seeking a new image of thought, or 'rather a liberation of thought from those images which imprison it'. In short he signals that even in the work of Guattari such a new image is the invocation of a 'vegetal' mode of thought; the rhizome in opposition to the tree, that is, a rhizome thought instead of an aborescent thought. In an interview he signals that chapter three of *Difference and Repetition* is the crucial chapter for understanding his work.

In the chapter entitled 'Difference in Itself', we find the concerted displacement of the problem of image and model in Plato, and thus what Deleuze creates is an affirmation of disjunction through a concept of difference, the same affirmation which informs *Schizophrenia and Capitalism*. Initially one could say it is posing the question of how sensibility, intelligibility and action are to be construed in a purer empiricism that can guide reflections here. Villani, in a bold effort to rescue Deleuze from charges of 'aestheticism', sees instead a way of arguing for what simply and clearly Deleuze says is his project: a search for a new philosophy of nature, and his goal, how to actually understand the science of the problem, and the creation of a new metaphysics which consists in the battle 'against neurosis and the typology of multiplicities'.[23]

One can see this as a rejection of a theory of mimesis based on the relation of image to a model, and instead an attending to the principles of nature, which can only be accomplished in a *focus imaginarius*. For Villani the central preoccupation in the work of Deleuze is 'that of isolating the conditions for the possibility of a complex act'. In some sense Villani wants to return agency to Deleuze and argue for a broader philosophical project within the creation itself, of concepts, of art, of new actions.

The second feature – the construction of the concept of the problem – is the one that Deleuze indicates as critical:

> I believe in the necessity of constructing a concept of the problem. I tried to do this in *Difference and Repetition* and would like to take up this question again. But practically speaking this approach has led me to ask, in each case, how a problem might be posed. It is in this manner, it seems to me, that philosophy might be considered a science: the science of determining the conditions of a problem.[24]

How indeed did Deleuze define the problem for philosophy? In answer to the question of Jean-Noel Vuranet, in 'On Nietzsche and the Image of Thought', Deleuze is clear and straightfor-

21 Steve Fuller, **Kuhn vs. Popper: The Struggle for the Soul of Science** (Columbia University Press, 2005).

22 Gilles Deleuze, **Difference and Repetition,** trans. Paul Patton (London: Continuum, 2004). First published by Presses Universitaires de France, Paris, as **Différence et Répétition**, 1968.

23 Arnaud Villani, '"I feel I am a pure metaphysician": The consequences of Deleuze's Affirmation', in **Collapse**, vol. III, November 2007, pp.45-63.

24 In **Collapse**, vol. III, November 2007.

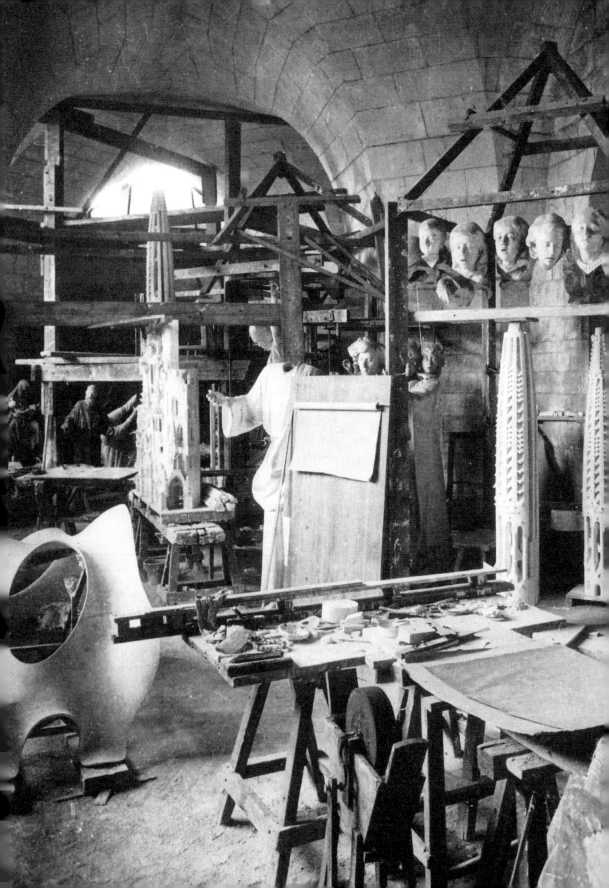

[1]

[4]

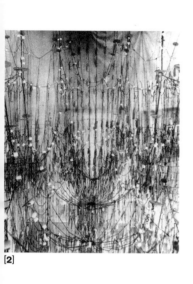

[2]

[5]

[3]

Antoni Gaudi, photo of the architect's
studio at the site of Sagrada Familia.
Antoni Gaudi, upside-down model of wires
and weights to determine the static relationships for Sagrada Familia.
Santiago Calatrava, model for I ponti di
Venezia, 1991.
4, 5 Santiago Calatrava, Athens Olympic
Sports Complex. Photo: G. Bruyns, 2006.

ward: the period of philosophy is a rich and confusing one, with no-one believing any more in the I, the Self, in characters or persons. The choice in philosophy between God and man, infinite substance or finite substance is no longer available: 'It is like Foucault said, we are no more human than God, the one dies with the other'.

For Deleuze, what we are discovering right now is a world packed with impersonal individuations, or even pre-individual singularities ('that's what Nietzsche means when he says "neither God nor man", its anarchy triumphant').[25]

The political implications of the loss of an assignable self, where fluidity enters, is that it cannot be policed or suppressed. Philosophy then for Deleuze 'must create worlds of thought, a whole new conception of thought', of what it means to think and it must be adequate to what is happening around us.

Deleuze reads the Platonic in a very particular way. How, one might ask, is the problem of the image and model to be found in Plato, which Deleuze tries to counter, and what are the consequences of that for the different artistic practices, especially architecture?

The tradition of the reading of the crucial text of Plato for this discussion, the *Timaeus*, is immense. Part of the hermeneutic problem is whether this dialogue is itself the delivery on Plato's own characterisation of his Socratic legacy, and also a return to an account of creation and the world modelled by a divine intelligence which is necessarily intelligible because it has been created by an intelligence which always, because of its goodness, resulted in the best world that is thinkable. The problem of the origin and cause of the world is raised also in Plato's account of Socrates, what constitutes an imputed autobiography, said to be delivered in prison shortly before his death. There Socrates spells out his effective rejection of pre-Socratic physics and the search for cause.[26]

The text in the *Phaedo* recounts that as a young man (probably around 450 BC) Socrates had sought the causes of things. It was natural science which attracted the young Socrates, as it was the science that had lofty aims and had to do with the cause of things, and that teaches why a thing is, and why it is created and destroyed. Socrates found himself incapable of such inquiries, and his studies had blinded him to his own awareness of things that he seemed to know, and others too, quite well. He had forgotten the self-evident by pursuing such questions as whether the brain was the originating power of perceptions, or whether we think with the blood, air, fire etc. In some sense Socrates recounts that he really cannot understand number and mathematical operations, that he couldn't satisfy himself that, when one is added to one, the one to which the addition is made becomes two, or that two units added together make two by reason of the addition.

Then, in this puzzled situation, he heard someone had a book of Anaxagoras, from which he reported that he had read that mind was the disposer and cause of all, which was a notion with which Socrates was delighted, as he found it admirable: 'I said to myself if mind is the disposer, mind will dispose all for the best, and put each particular in the best place, things that exist now and things that have yet to exist. They are all arranged by intelligence'.

It is, of course, arguable that this cosmic creating and cognitively capable intelligence is other than that of which we are possessed. However in the constructivist paradigm, which also echoes that of the craftsman Hephaestus in Hesiod's account of the creation of woman (*Works and Days*, 59-68), the world is made by *nous* and human beings may be the best repository for the activities of *nous* as it arranges world, and worlds. The arrangement of the world is itself an architecture of *nous*.

The consideration of a causal principle, called *nous* in Anaxagoras, with *nous*, translatable as 'mind', 'intelligence', is regarded as something infinite and autonomous and crucially not mixed with anything else, alone and by itself. It is this being alone by itself that allows it to control other things.[27] This is also how it is designated as the causal principle *par excellence*. It also has a directive awareness, because of the things which are being mixed, separated and segregated, Anaxagoras says, *nous* 'knew all of them', what they would become and what they were. One could say the account of Anaxagoras shows how the various ingredients of the world are mixed together, and the world was once so compact and homogenous that there was no difference.

Because of *nous* a vortex has been created in which the ingredients are separated out and divided, and according to different proportions, even though there is a portion of everything in everything, and only the weight of proportionality determines what a thing is, that is, whatever the predominant part of the mixture is called. Selecting and determining are intrinsic actions of intelligibility and the intelligible.

It was with this promissory note from Anaxagoras that Socrates hoped to be shown the causes of existence. He could now discover if the earth was flat or round, and could learn then the nature of the best, and show how this was the best. He thought that he might then have answers to questions not just about the earth, but the sun, moon and stars, and how their movements and returnings to various states would be the best. Since mind was the disposer, what account could one give that did not assert this was the best? He would learn what was the best for each and what was the best for all.

Socrates plunged into reading the books, and was grievously disappointed. He found the philosopher altogether forsaking mind or any other principle of order, and having recourse to air and ether, and water, 'and other eccentricities'. These become in Socrates' account a parody of reductive thinking, because the account is like someone saying that mind is the cause of Socrates – waiting in prison to take the hemlock – but then explains the cause of action by attributing it

25 G. Deleuze, **Desert Islands and Other Texts, 1953-1974**, ed. D. Lapoujade, trans. Michael Taormina (Los Angeles: Semiotext(e) Foreign Agents Series, 2004), pp.135-142.
26 Plato, **Complete Works**, ed. J.M. Cooper (Indianapolis: Hackett Publishing Company, 1997). **Phaedo**, trans. G.M.A. Grube, (pp.49-101, 96b-101e). At pages 85-87 in Grube's translation.
27 For this see: G.S. Kirk & J.E. Raven, **The Presocratic Philosophers** (Cambridge: Cambridge University Press, 1957), chapter XV, pp.362-394.

to the body made of bones and muscles, and describing the bones and their ability to contract and relax as the explanation. Then he could explain this talking by Socrates to Cebes in the prison as to do with sound and air and hearing, mentioning ten thousand other causes of the same sort, and not mentioning the true cause, 'that the Athenians have sought fit to condemn me'. This is a confusion of cause and condition; obviously without bones and muscles one cannot execute one's purpose, but to say that one does something because of them, and that this is the way the mind acts, is a very careless and idle mode of speaking.

'I wonder that they cannot distinguish the cause from the condition which the many feeling about in the dark are always mistaking and misnaming'. Socrates admits that he has failed to discover himself or to learn of anyone else the nature of the best, and offers to exhibit what he has found to be the second best mode of inquiring into the cause:

> I thought that as I had failed in the contemplation of true existence, I ought to be careful that I did not lose the eye of my soul; as people may injure their bodily eye by observing and gazing on the sun during an eclipse, unless they take the precaution of only looking at the image (eikon) reflected in the water, or in some similar medium. This occurred to me, and I was afraid that my soul might be blinded altogether if I looked at things with my eyes or tried by the help of the senses to apprehend them. I thought that I had better have recourse to ideas, and seek in them the truth of existence.[28]

Socrates acknowledges that the simile is not perfect, as he does not want to admit that someone who contemplates existence through the medium of ideas sees them only 'through a glass darkly' any more than he sees them in their working and effects.

However, he says that was the method he adopted; he assumed some principle which he judged to be the strongest, and then affirmed as true whatever seemed to agree with this, whether relating to the cause or to anything else, and that which disagreed he regarded as untrue.

Plato included in the *Phaedo* a myth which offers a view that the spherical is significant for the shape of the earth and surrounding heavens, and emphasises that it is at rest because of symmetry. Above the surface there are places underwater, some in the air, and some in the upper reaches of the aether. This tripartite division is also relevant to the assignation of the purification of souls, which rise from Tartarus where they undergo punishment, through being incarnated in the upper region, where they attain purity.

The myth avoids the need for the elements to be given a causal power, and other eccentricities; instead there is an intelligent making which corresponds to the journey or purification and exemplification available for soul. It clearly displays a Pythagorean source.

The speech of Timaeus is the main source for the powerful metaphysical disjunction between a realm of intelligible being, separate from and even opposed to perceptible becoming. When trying to explain the world of perceptible becoming, it is necessary to deal in degrees of likelihood as to explanation. It is not possible to have the certitude which can be gained from changeless entities.

The reflections which Socrates left are re-engaged by Plato in the *Timaeus*. Timaeus delivers his exposition in a dry and pedantic tone, with the slight boredom of someone who has again to repeat truths to the uncomprehending. He begins with a proposition that can also be found in *Republic* and *Laws*, namely that the visible world is necessarily made after a model. One can think in fact of two models which are entailed by the primary disjunction between the sensible and the intelligible, a model which is always existent and does not become, and one which strictly speaking never is, and never ceases to come into being:

> As I see it then we must begin by making the following distinctions: What is that which always is and has no becoming, and what is that which becomes but never is? The former is grasped by the understanding, which involves a reasoned account. It is unchanging. The latter is grasped by opinion which involves unreasoning sense perception. Now whatever comes to be must of necessity come to be by the agency of some cause, for it is impossible for anything to come to be without a cause. So whenever the craftsman (demiourgos) looks at what is always changeless and, using a thing of that kind as his model, reproduces its form and character, then of necessity, all that he so completes is beautiful. But were he to look at a thing that has come to be and use as his model something that has been begotten, his work will lack beauty … Well if this world of ours is beautiful, and its craftsman good, then clearly he looked at the eternal model.
> (*Timaeus*, 27d; 28a-c; 29a-b)

In *Republic* v, 472, the reality of the idea of Justice is shown to involve necessarily a model of Justice:

> Then it was in order to have a model that we were trying to discover what justice itself is like.

And at 472d:

> Do you think that someone is a worse painter, if having presented a model of what the finest and most beautiful human being would be like, and having rendered every detail of his picture adequately, he could not prove that such a man could come into being?

Silver stater from Knossos (diameter
25mm), c. 350-325 BC.

And again, at 472e:

> Then what about our own case? Didn't we say we were making a theoretical model of a good city?

This echoes the passage at *Republic* II, 369 c:

> Come then, let us create a city in theory from its beginnings.

Every craftsman works from an original, and thus always makes a copy. In fact the account in the *Timaeus*, which is said to be given the day after the *Republic*, is linked to the problem of the paradigm and model, in a way that is crucial to follow, namely the way in which the model and paradigm itself literally functioned in and dominated Greek life. The different paradigms of the divine and of nature for human life are reconstituted by Plato to exhibit the maximum structural and intellectual intelligibility.

Leaving aside the direct Pythagorean provenance, the clear implication is that this account runs against the notions inherited from the epic tradition, and also re-situates the relation of the divine and human. Why, we might ask, is the divine maker a carpenter? Also, how do models work and interact in the historical and political life of the Greeks?

Once again we can see that the early role of the mythic and the epic had been emblematic in Greek culture, indeed is what eventually allowed a Greek culture to emerge. The point about myth was already noted by Jaeger in his *Paideia*: 'The myth, the heroic legend is the inexhaustible reservoir of models which the nation possesses and from which its thought derives ideals and norms for its own life'.[29] Even the conception of making and production had an emblematic and paradigmatic myth, one of enormous complexity and ambivalence, which is literally counter-modelled in the activity of the Demiurgos, or Demiurge. It is of course the story of the creations of Daedalus, the wooden cow, the labyrinth, and the wings which he makes to enable his son to fly away from Crete, that is, the exemplum of the creative fabricator.

Pasiphae's deception of the bull with the full co-operation of Daedalus leads to the birth of the Minotaur, which results in a construction that needs to be built to pen in the monster. A cunning construction is needed to effect the seduction, and another to hide its monstrous consequences. More significant than the entire web of deceptions, illusions and betrayal which emanate from the 'lying island' is that the Labyrinth itself is the emblem of the work of the artist, artifex, creator.[30] The maze as constructed serves for the model which Hephaestus works on the shield of Achilles. Here there is a dense weave of allusion and reference. Hephaestus is the craftsman responsible for the creation of Pandora, but the Homeric reference to the dance floor

29 Werner Jaeger, **Paideia** (Oxford: Oxford University Press, 1986). First published in German in 1934. **The Theology of Early Greek Philosophers** (Oxford: Oxford University Press, 1947).
30 For a fascinating analysis of this material, see: Rebecca Armstrong, **Cretan Women** (Oxford: Oxford University Press, 2006), pp.124-166.

made on Achilles' shield is attributed to a human model, and not, as the epic normally requires, the reverse.

The suggestion of Steven Lonsdale in his *Dance and Ritual Play in Greek Religion* is fascinating in this context, namely that Hephaestus is something of an outsider among the Olympians, his lameness and ugliness being the subject of Olympian humour and his ugliness having been the cause of his lameness, as his mother, Hera, on seeing his appearance as a baby threw him from the Olympian heights, thus maiming him for life. He has his revenge on his mother through a complex invisible device which enchains her in her throne, from which the other gods cannot release her.[31]

Dionysus gets Haephaestus in his cups, and Hera is freed. Lonsdale analyses the depiction of the Return to Olympia on vase paintings, showing the figure on a mule, and argues that the myth of the maiming and return of Hephaestus belongs, broadly speaking, to the topsy-turvy world of reversals celebrating the triumph of the oppressed. It is a paradigm of festivals of reversal in the social order in archaic and classical Greece, elements of which can be glimpsed in festivals such as the Athenian Anthesteria.[32]

The famous limping god engraved a dance floor, like the one made by Daedalus in broad Conossus, for lovely-haired Ariadne (*Iliad*, 18, 590-2). The term for dance floor is *chorus*, but it also means the place, the dancers, or the activity. It is probably Minoan in origin. Having reviewed the etymological discussions, Lonsdale suggests the essential meaning is probably spatial and indicates that which is open, so that a city with such a space is also open.

However, the fame achieved by humans in their deeds and making, *kleos*, is always less than that of the immortal gods. Odysseus even warns against any confusion on this matter. The hero can be a model, as can the past. Inevitably the imitator is inferior to the model, and thus the dance floor/shield contain a deadly ambivalence for these claims.

The shield of Achilles has also been deciphered by Giesecke as itself a model of the cosmos.[33] She develops a utopian reading of the *Odyssey*, where the dystopian 'society' of the Cyclops marks the extreme condition: for them there is neither 'deliberating assemblies nor precedents of law', or further, 'each makes his own law over his children and wives, and for one another they have no regards' (*Odyssey* 9, 105-115). Aristotle takes them as the outstanding example of

31 Steven Lonsdale, **Dance and Ritual Play in Greek Religion** (Baltimore and London: The Johns Hopkins University Press, 1993).

32 Lonsdale, **ibid.**, p.88 and p.118.

33 Annete L. Giesecke, **The Epic City** (Center for Hellenic Studies, Harvard, 2007). See also my 'Pollachos Polis Legetai (There are Many Ways to Say Polis); or: Community and the Visible of the City', in **Visualizing The Invisible**, eds. S. Read and C. Pinilla (Amsterdam: Techne Press, 2006), pp.21-31.

 Corbusier, original model of Musée à
issance illimitée, version for Philippeville,
eria, 1939.

the a-political, because they lack the hearth, and are thus marked out as in-human, bestial and not fit for the life of the city.

On the island of Calypso, Odysseus comes face to face with the 'animate myth of matriarchy'. Ulysses is wiled into sleeping with Calypso but is frightened by her range of skills and aware of her self-reliance and seeks to be gone. In the encounter with Circe there is an explicit ideological confrontation between male and female, provoking violence in the male, because Circe is the greatest threat to evolved patriarchal civilisation. Circe lives in a stone polished house, her architectonic faculties suggesting, as Giesecke notes, that she has progressed well into the province that Western culture has claimed as masculine. Her remarkable skill at weaving constitutes 'an architecture', the skill at making clothing, which is a primal shelter.

All the other meetings, those with the Lotus Eaters and the descent into Hades, remain unappealing to Odysseus, as they are ways of life that exist without the security of the city. From Giesecke's reading the *Odyssey* must be considered as utopian, and she thinks it not inappropriate to see Odysseus' re-organisation on his return to Ithaca as a metaphorical, mythological re-enacting of Greece's historical evolution from the order of Mycenaean palace-based society through the chaos of the Dark Age to an urban, polis-based society. From his various visits, it is the polis of the Phaiakians which Odysseus takes home.

This is a utopian model, and the poems of Homer can be read as a paradigm for seeing and talking about the world. In the poems the view is expressed that the polis is the place of civilised living, progress, justice, community, openness. Aristotle supports the Homeric model, saying that the polis came into being 'for the purpose of promoting good living' (*Politics* 1252b, 29-30). The struggle of Hector and Achilles is then a struggle over the normative values of the polis. Figured at the centre of the shield are *poleis kalas*, two cities: the cities of war and peace (*Iliad* 8, 490-91).

However, the instability of the various paradigm interactions is no doubt something Plato sets out to counter. As Capizzi has pointed out in great detail, the heroic model is andric.[34] The hero is indeed *aristos*, the best. It further entails a courageous and noble disposition. Achilles is the prototype, who in learning compassion for the slayer of his companion will at the end of the *Iliad* acquire the heroic greatness to live in the City of Peace. Equally the past is presented as a paradigm and promoted for the present.

The figure of Nestor incarnates this model, he has the duty of communicating the paradigmatic status of one generation to the next, and the role of the paradigmatic myth is to improve the present. However, the past is not endless and human genealogy only takes one so far; ultimately it is with a god or gods that genealogies begin. The gods are the ultimate source of *kleos*.

One then has the case of a super-paradigm, which transcends time, finding its own end in eternity. This is the divine model of human actions – which actually transfers as the paradigm of royalty. The other great paradigm is nature. However, another disjunction is already inscribed, and one that bears on the exemplary place of the city for Greek experience. The order of the city is man-made, and nature cannot be considered as 'productive'.

There is a paradigmatic city which does not share so directly the epic inheritance and which has no mythic origin. This is Sparta. It is the ideal city which finds its own reality of sufficient paradigmatic significance. The figuring on the shield and the model of Sparta encompass a vast range of conflicting and different claims, which point to the highly political aspect of all such models. It is also a drastic contrast with the Homeric world of dispute between kings and heroes. Capizzi has the most suggestive account: each personal connotation is cancelled out, and the bosses themselves are basically so many slaves of the community, which together they all make up, becoming bosses only if seen from the outside; the sacrifice of all for the honour of one, the case of Achilles, is reversed in Sparta where the sacrifice of each for the salvation of all is the first and most solid principle of Spartan *paideia*.

Megara, Argos and Corinth are certainly paler versions of the principle, but precisely for this reason they are also proofs of its paradigmatic nature. The world of archaic peninsular Greece has no need of mythical paradigms because it has a real one: Sparta, the collective hero, the city whose real king (as Pindar will one day sing) is law itself.

Jaeger and Gaetano de Sanctis both point to the fact that the paradigm is not the mythical abstraction of the ancients god or heroes but the living presence of the Spartan hoplite phalanx, providing a 'model' where agonistic values are transcended and the ethical and communitarian motive is emphasised.

With exquisite tenderness, Virgil sings of the Labyrinth, the daedalian fabrications and the complex model of human making:

> Hic crudelis amor tauri suppostaque furto,
> …
> hic labor ille domus et inextricabilis error;
> magnum reginae sed enim miseratus amorem
> Daedalus ipse dolos tecti ambagesque resoluit,
> caeca regens filo vestigia. (*Aeneid*, 6, 442)

The adjective 'crudelis' here makes of the queen an unhappy lover.

Rebecca Armstrong suggests that this may be the reason for Daedalus's sympathy, and the motivating source of his provision for the solution of the maze. His pity extends to both mother and daughter, Pasiphae and Ariadne, and to that drama of woman's passion for a bull, a minotaur

34 Antonio Capizzi, **The Cosmic Republic** (Amsterdam: Gieben, 1990).

who fails to play the part of the monster, and the love affair of Theseus and Ariadne, who remain unnamed while Daedalus holds the guiding thread.

Daedalus solved the tricks and windings of the building. The ingenious craftsman, architect, 'guiding blind steps with a thread'. Clement of Alexandria, who tittle-tattled on the Greek mysteries as a pagan convert to Christianity, suggests in his *Protrepticus*, 4: 'And the cow of Daedalus made of wood, fooled a wild bull, and art deceived and forced the beast into mounting a woman in love'.

Ovid manages to write about the Labyrinth and elide the distinction between the order of nature and the human order. By an act of trickery, a sleight of hand, Daedalus famous for the genius of the craftsman's art, built the work and confused the signs. Daedalus is compared to the watery river Meander, twisting forward and backwards in confusing flow and meeting itself as it sees its own waters coming up. It busies its confused waters, just so had Daedalus filled countless paths with wandering and hardly managed to get back to the threshold; so great was the trickery of the building:

Ita Daedalus implet
innumeras errore uias uicque ipse reuerti
ad limen potuit: tanta est fallacia tecti.

(Ovid, *Metamorphoses*, 8, 159-1698).

It is taken as one of the deepest paradoxes of Plato that the importance of the notion of the image in his work coincides with its complete condemnation. The figure of the subterfuge and deceit of Daedalus stalks the work of Plato, and is taken as the greatest inhibition to a knowledge of the truth of things as they are, *aletheia ton onton* (*Phaedo*, 99e) or the truth of things, *aletheia ton pragmaton* (*Sophist*, 234c). To produce a true discourse, to say what things really are, means that one must not rest content with resemblances. To think things as they are, means that one cannot confuse things and their appearance, truth and its images. The act of research in Plato of the truth means sorting out the semblance from the real, identifying that which is a false resemblance. However there is a further consideration: the image is not just a false semblance, it is mobilised to underline the more complex situation of sensible knowledge.[35] Grasso has pertinently asked why, given the clear opposition between an immutable identity in itself and the relativising consequences of flux, Plato had recourse to the 'image'.[36]

The image is not reduced to simply 'faux semblant'. It permits one to devalue the sensible, but also to save it. Plato affirms the transcendence and separation of the Form, but is also concerned to establish the reality of its relation to things below, which are not other than its resemblance. The image is not the model, but is what is appropriate to every *eidolon*. It is an 'other', similar to the original.

It is a *heteron toiouton* (*Sophist*, 240a). So an image of the model seems to appear as if it has no being, and yet must of necessity be in a certain manner like the model:

Theaetetus: What in the world would we say a copy is, sir, except something that's made similar to a true thing and is another thing that's like it?
Visitor: You're saying it's another true thing like it? Or what do you mean by like it?
Theaetetus: Not that it's true at all, but that it resembles the true thing.
Visitor: Meaning by true, really being?
Theaetetus: Yes.
Visitor: And meaning by not true, contrary of true?
Theaetetus: Of course.
Visitor: So you are saying that that which is like is not really that which is, if you speak of it as not true.
Theaetetus: But it is, in a way.
Visitor: But not truly, you say.
Theaetetus: No, except that it really is a likeness.
Visitor: So it is not really what is, but it really is what we call a likeness?
Theaetetus: Maybe that which is not is woven together with that which is in some way like that – it is quite bizarre.

These characteristics assure the sensible of a minimum of consistency; the *pragmata* by their participation in the Forms receive a minimum determination which anchors their identity as things and their being capable of being thought. Insofar as they participate in this or that form, they can be thought of in such and such a way, and not in every and any way all at the same time. Such an infinity of determinations would be the strict equivalent of the absence of any true determination. Grasso argues that by recourse to the relation between image and model Plato can give all his support to the relation between two orders of 'reality', one of which is true, and which penetrates the second completely, and this grants intelligibility which escapes the onto-logical catastrophe of a pure flux of Heraclitus, or the obdurate phenomenism of Protogoras.

Through the scheme of the image the sensible is granted its enabling intelligibility. From this one can gather the troubling strangeness of the image in the passage from the *Sophist*.

From reading the passage in the *Cratylus* it is clear that the image does not have to resemble in every point. To do so would mean that it becomes a double. To be an image of something it must resemble and not resemble at the same time. With the *Sophist* there is a further reflection on the status of the image, where it is taken as made in the resemblance of the true.

The use of the term *eidolon* suggests that which approaches or reproduces sufficiently the

35 Elsa Grasso, 'Platon ou l'aurore des idoles', in **L'image**, ed. Alexander Schnell (Paris: Vrin, 2007), pp.9-30.
36 This view is also supported in a key study of the Platonic material by Peter Brommer, **Eidos et Idea** (Assen: Van Gorcum, 1940). The author tends strongly to interpret **eidos** as structure, which belongs to Plato's saving of appearances for 'the real', and ultimately the really real, which is the Good in itself.

original so that the 'alterity', the relation of resembling and not resembling, is based on the 'same' and the 'similar', which characterised the real relation between them. The term from its archaic usage is often distinguished from *eidos* in a firmer way than in the Platonic corpus. In Homer it has the sense of ghostly, evanescent, something intuited about things seen which exist but are not directly known, what might be called a weak viewing. Perhaps the sense of 'ghostly' is the closest to the archaic usage in Greek. At *Odyssey* 4, 824, Athena assumes the appearance of Penelope's sister in what is described as a 'dim likeness', *eidolon amauron*.

In the usage of *eidos* there is a fuller force of communication and immediacy. The power of the image has the ability to stun and amaze, it also is capable of inducing wonder, and belongs to the realm of appearance. The further sense is that it is arresting. The gods can make an *eidos* appear, as for example in *Odyssey* 4, 12-14: 'The gods did not cause to appear any further offspring after she gave birth to the lovely child Hermione, who has the shape/form – *eidos* – of golden Aphrodite'. In the *Iliad* 3, 224 the relation to the sense of a sublime response is indicated, in the wonder expressed by those who gaze upon the *eidos* of Odysseus: *hod Odyseos agassamet eidos idontes*.

The philosophical problem which arises is: what is the path that leads from the notion of image to the thinking of *logos* itself? And indeed, further: how in the realm of the sensible does image enter into an act of thought? What one may say is at stake, is the way in which intelligible relations can be expressed *per se*, of which the most eminent objects are the Forms themselves. From the *Republic* VI, 511, the properly philosophical *logos* in its most developed part of the 'line' attaches itself to intelligibility through the power of *logos*, or discourse:

> There are these two things, one sovereign of the intelligible kind and place, the other of the visible … In any case you have two kinds of things, visible and intelligible … It is like a line divided into two unequal sections. Then divide each section – namely that of the visible and that of the intelligible – in the same ratio as the line. In terms of relative clarity and opacity, one subsection of the visible consists of images. And by images I mean, first, shadows, then reflections in water and in all close-packed, smooth and shiny materials, and everything of that sort, if you understand … In the other subsection of the visible put the original of these images, namely, the animals around us, all the plants, and the whole class of manufactured things … Consider now how the section of the intelligible is to be divided … In one subsection, the soul using as images the things that were imitated before, is forced to investigate from hypotheses, proceeding not to a first principle but to a conclusion. In the other subsection, however, it makes its way to a first principle that is not an hypothesis, proceeding from an hypothesis but without the images used in the previous subsection, using forms themselves and

making its investigation through them.
(*Republic*, VI, 509d-510b-d).

A further enhancement of the power of the image is given in the *Sophist*, where it is invoked as making possible the rendering of the distinction between true and false *logos*; part of the intense difficulty of defining the sophist from the true philosopher is exactly the ability of the sophist to seem and dissemble, and look like the real and the true. Sophistry is not so much the art of skilful technical deployment within the field of rhetoric and persuasion, but rather it is the elusive and always artful resemblance to what in fact it is not. This is the way in which the *eidolon* is then also a notion of image but with a connotation of irreality. It belongs to the lexical group which includes *eidos*, and is understood as aspect, or visible form, which is ultimately rooted in a thematic root expressing the idea of seeing. Whilst it is the case in Homer that it can belong to the weightless idea of the image within a dream, or of supernatural apparition, it is also the case that in almost all cases it is a form drained of depth, which has an almost perfect resemblance to its model.

Grasso, following the reading of Jean-Paul Vernant, gives the archaic sense another complexion, suggesting that it is not a mental product, or a representation, but more, indeed, an apparition, possessed of a reality of belonging to an inaccessible elsewhere.[37] The fact that it is deprived of material consistency appropriate to everyday realities means that the *eidolon* is compared to escaping smoke for those who want to capture it.

The problem of the visible and invisible meet in the image, and cannot be understood without abandoning the conceptual language which is a language of daytime. Light belongs to the being of the world. The thinking which cannot look directly upon the source of visibility is constrained to look through shadows and reflections. The possibility of such advertence is itself granted by source itself, which is the ever-active making present both of place and boundary and position for human knowing. Even in the notion of *logos* as discourse there is the active manifestation, which is as much an irradiance as it is the making seen from what is said to exist.

Seeing is granted by visibility, which is granted by light and the sun. The look of the eye is glancing, gleaming, sharp and capable of being ferocious. The extraordinary simile in Homer of the mountain snake fed on evil drugs awaiting a man in his lair, with grim anger entering him, shooting his terrible glance, speaks vividly. The gleam of the eye is the power of ferocious capture, it signals primal force. Everything is caught within it. The look can also be all-appearing. Light is enervating, destructive and beautiful, it is capable of ordering and locating through its movement, even dying is a place where the horizon becomes the fundamental condition of the boundary, from which everything proceeds again. Thus also the dawn is a place of revelation, and night and darkness the setting for what is mortal.[38]

---

37 Jean Paul Vernant, 'Figuration de l'invisible et catégorie psychologique du double: le colossos', **Myths et pensée chez les Grecs: Etudes de psychologie historique** (Paris: La Découverte, 1996), pp.329-330.
38 Raymond A. Prier, **Thauma Idesthai** (Tallahassee: Florida State University Press, 1989).

What can be observed is a general vocabulary in Homer of appearing and specific platial and spatial features that emerge from the granting that occurs with the sun's own appearance. Again, Achilles with his cunningly wrought war instrument, when running down Hector, emits brazen light and is a force of light as appearance, even if the light of appearance is from the other world. The sun, as the god Helios, grants appearance itself, it is all-appearing. Through its shining it places and locates, it reveals objects of importance. At *Iliad* 3, in the call of Agamemnon it is invoked as that which 'sees and hears all'. Perhaps the synaesthesia offers more than we can simply understand. There is a revealing of the boundaries of the world in the granting of appearance, otherwise one is completely lost.

Perhaps the most revealing passage of all, in which the light of the sun, the moon and the stars, and the fire and brightness of the microcosmos are gathered is that of *Iliad* 8, 555-63:

> As when in the heavens around the appearing moon the stars seems bright for themselves, the air is still, all the lookout hills and high headlands and valleys appear, and from the direction of the heavens the unspeakably great aether was cleft, and all stars were seen, and the shepherd is mindful with gladness, so many fires appeared for themselves, between the ships and the streams of Xanthus when the Trojans kindled them before Ilium. A thousand fires were burning in the plain, and by each sat fifty in the gleaming beam of the blazing fire.

What seems most significant in terms of Plato's treatment of *eidolon* and *eidos* is in the case of *eidolon,* which in Homer is often related to and identical with a psyche deprived of a body, whereas with Plato it is very much caught up in the *soma,* the body. *Eidolon* is also characterised as an appearance offered to the look, for example of a bed which a painter takes as a model. The essential character isolated by Plato can be taken as visibility. However, Plato's uses of the term also bring together all kinds of things in different domains that can be said to appear to be: one can talk of the false *eidolon* of *techne,* or of the political (*Gorgias,* 463 d-e). One can also apply this to false or illusory virtues in which the crowd believes and which the poets, his own contemporaries are meant, reproduce, and fake pleasures (*Republic,* x; *Republic,* ix, 587c, 587d), and to apparent knowledge (*Theaetetus,* 150b, 150e, 152c). Written discourse which can be a pale reflection of *logos* which lives and breathes in the soul is an *eidolon* (*Phaedrus,* 276a).

In some way the otherness of the *eidolon,* from archaic usage, which is still similar in the relation to the real has lost its sense of apparition, and becomes a pure apparition implying an essential non-being, and effectively as Grasso comments: 'l'apparition devient image'. This implies further that there is a disqualification on the part of Plato where he links *eidolon* to *eidos* in a novel way.

The genealogy of both terms with their common sense in visibility gives way to a determination of the first as a degradation of the second, the latter which was inscribed originally in the order of the sensible becomes that form which can only be seen with the 'eye' of the soul.

There is a new disjunction, an opposition between *eidolon*, sometimes visible and always distinct from intelligible beings, and *eidos* which is now inscribed in participation. Things below are only *eidola* (*Phaedrus*, 250 d 5). The text of *Phaedrus* also suggests that, as reflections calling on Form, they call on an original from which they derive, and which is treated as a model, but their status is highly ambivalent with the possibility of being led towards that from which they depart, or indicate it in a kind of memoration.

Such a relation is as much separation as unity, and it is explicitly called mimetic; for example, *eidolon* is the product of artistic mimesis in the *Republic*, and in the *Sophist* one also finds the term *eidolopoiike*, which one can translate as the fabrication of images, and is directly identified with *mimetike*. The terms which designate the products of *mimetike* are *eikon* and *phantasmata*, and the most frequent usage in the corpus of mimesis applies to the artistic field. Such an application has distant roots, and perhaps most obviously return to the *chora* of the dance and mime associated with the Daedalian labyrinth.

They must also relate to imitation, with gestures and attitude and voice, and probably to ritualised drama; however, the indication is that they should be understood as dynamic representation and not inanimate things produced in a static fashion. Here it can be noted that it is Plato who is the first to apply mimesis in such a broad way to all the arts, not just to music or poetry but also to sculpture.

He also serves the term in contexts outside of art and in a diverse, plural way. In the *Timaeus* (50c-51b), there is a usage which applies to human activities which behave as something else, and even sensible things in general. Political constitutions, discourse, words and even the effort of the philosopher who tries to make himself similar to intelligible beings (*Cratylus*, 423c; *Republic* VI, 500c).

Through these examples one can see that the original comprehension of mimesis has undergone a fundamental transformation. The relation is no longer that of the imitator to that which is seen or heard, but it is above all because of the new perspective offered by Plato that mimetic products are now granted an inferior value, which is expressed with the terms *eidolon* and *phantasma*.

Phantasma is inseparable form the idea of appearance, belonging to the lexical group of *phaino* which means show, or show itself, or appear and reveal as in the middle voice of *phainesthai*, seems, appear as and so on. In a sense the English 'phantom' comes close to the new implication in Plato, with meanings of irreality, and in this case tied to the problem of reflection, artistic image, or an appearance for a subject, which can be a 'phenomenon', especially the image of a dream, or as in the *Timaeus*, that which impresses itself through the senses on the liver, which is linked to divination (*Timaeus*, 46a, 71a, 71c, 71e).

However, crucially we can also find in Plato the idea of the image as the manifestation of the thing as it is. The character of resemblance is understood as a conforming to something and this substitutes the notion of appearance as attached to the older meaning of *eidolon*, or is added to the general idea as signified by the use of *mimema* of production or of imitation.

So, what is stressed is now conformity, what might be termed a just fit, and *eikon* has then an essential relation to the idea of a model, to which it can precisely correspond. In the writings of Plato this value is granted through the first sense, and not just in the artistic domain, but also in the discursive, and above all in the cosmological order.

The inferior degree of participation of images in truth can be placed at the epistemological and ontological level. Objects that are images participate less in truth. A state of soul is granted clarity or certainty superior to that which preceded it because it has abandoned images for their original, especially in the case of belief and knowing, or because it treats the *eikones* as copies and not as originals. The relation of intellect to opinion is the same as that of being to becoming. *Eikones* and *phantasmata* are at the lowest level of the ontological hierarchy. Even in the education of the guardians in the allegory of the cave there is a stress on the inferiority of the image.

The movement of knowledge is figured as a movement of successive vision, vision on vision, visions of images less and less removed from their origin; the first are the shadow of *eidola* fashioned by man, the last is the reflection seen in the full light and is of divine making, that is *phantasmata theia* (*Republic*, VII, 532c). Thus, as in the account of Visitor, the notion of the image is a degradation from an original, from the original and intelligible model, and only the *logos* can give an adequate account of this. Thus, the reproduction of things not as they are, but as they appear, is a mimesis not of *aletheia*, nor of a material entity, but of what manifests itself as apparition (*Republic*, 598a). No *eidola* or *phantasmata* can show or demonstrate the intelligible model. Grasso makes the strong point that there is really no passage in Plato which indicates clearly that works of art can be viewed as images of the Forms.[39]

Critically, in the *Cratylus* we must do research that departs from *eidola* and *phantasmata* to the onomastic image. Naming is treated as stating, and the question arises whether names and their correct assignments depend on their descriptive content. What makes up the *logos* of a sentence is, according to the *Sophist*, the weaving together of names with verbs and predicates of expression, that is also the sense of *nooma* as agents, *rhema* showing actions performed by agents. It is possible to say true or false names. Can one avoid incorrect names by having a correct conceptual schema? The fundamental tension may be between naturalism and conventionalism. Names speak things as they are, or it is a matter of correct use and convention. The argument of Hermogenes is that names do not exist by nature but by law and custom, their correctness is by convention. Socrates shows that this subjectivism, which we have seen in Nietzsche's view of language, makes it impossible to distinguish between true and false. For Socrates there is a necessity to show that there are objectively correct names, there are real things which occupy a place and position. It is not a question of one's own will, but the method and tool prescribed by the nature of things that must be employed. In that sense the name is a kind of tool. There is a model correct name, which is a translinguistic entity which cannot be identified with any sounds or marks.

Kretzmann argues this succinctly: the actual name is a correct name, in the sense that there ought to be such a name in use, if and only if that name is an embodiment in sounds or marks of the model correct name of x;[40] that is: 1) there are x's; 2) the name is used or intended to be used as a name for x; and 3) there is a model correct name of x. There is a model correct name of x if, and only if, there is a Form as x, and secondly there is a logically proper name of that Form which is embodied in sounds or marks. The correctness of the model correct name of x is natural in that it copies the form of x, at least to the extent that it includes enough essential features of x, features constitutive of the Form of x, so that it could not also be the name of some other form, and secondly, it excludes all individuating features of any single x, and all differentiating features of any sub-group of x.

Socrates, at 391 a-b, observes that something already appears that we were looking for, something we did not know before; that names have a certain natural correctness, and that not every man knows how to give a name well to anything whatever. Correctness implies that the actual names have been imposed by the appropriate law-giver operating on principles and models supplied by the dialectician. This activity of the *nomothetes* is the human equivalent of the divine *demiourgos*.

Perspicuous embodiment discloses the model correct name and therefore points to the form which the model correct name copies and in which the bearers of the actual name participate. This indicates that names are conventional, in that there is a name giver, but not conventional in that there is a naturally correct name. Names are an instrument or tool whose function is to separate and classify things according to their nature. This requires expertise in order to discover the taxonomy relevant to a certain subject. The dialectician is the expert at dividing reality. The phonetic unit reveals the nature of things if and only if the elements of the phonetic unit correspond to and imitate *mimesthai* the nature of things.

From 424c we could argue that language can be an imitation *mimema* or picture *eikon* of the world. The primitive relation between language and world is that of naming. At 436b however, Socrates cautions that whoever follows names and examines into the meaning of each one runs great risks of being deceived, and he argues against ordinary language accounts, and also against Formalism.

---

39 See note 35.
40 Norman Kretzmann, 'Plato on the correctness of names', in **American Philosophical Quarterly**, 8, 1971, pp.126-138.

There is also a need for a direct acquaintance with things, what might be characterised as a natural metaphysics of things. Learning about things depends on understanding that the world is a place of given articulations and necessary connections, it is textured and has thickness throughout. To have particular essential properties usually entails membership of a kind, but the converse is not true. At 387d, sensible concrete particulars and actions have their own being and special nature, *auton tino idion phusin*. What is significant is that language itself separates out features of reality as the shuttle separates out the warp and the woof, and definitions become and are complex images of reality. Names are conventional and disclose things to those who establish convention that, if changed, is still correct. There is no difference as to what convention is adopted.

In the *Timaeus* the world is determined as image and at the same time 'the best, most excellent, beautiful' (*Timaeus*, 92c). Where the conformity of the *eikon* is evaluated it designates the world of sensible realities. The nouns *mimesis* and *mimema* are used for the work of the divine *demiourgos* as a production of images, a second degree of being subject to becoming, and the visible is a *mimema paradeigmatos*, an imitation of a model, 'intelligible and remaining always the same' (*Timaeus*, 48e-49a). Although of the second rank, it is still a positive evaluation of the image, as it applies to the work of the whole and also to real particulars.

The activity of the *demiourgos* is to exercise a looking on the model, *paradeigma*. The excellence of the model chosen by the demiourgos confers an undeniable value on the image, which is emphasised throughout the dialogue and especially at the beginning. The argument also works in the other direction: the very beauty of the world and the goodness of its maker witness clearly a looking towards the eternal model.

In the *Sophist*, two forms and two values of the image are indicated and other distinctions are developed. We have the example of two kinds of *eidola* representing mimetic operations according to the same model, and the distinction drawn is between clear representation and illusory appearance. Here the rendering is considered as unlike, for the *eikon* conforms to the proportions of its model, its *summetria* is one of perfectly resembling or more precisely the similar and the same, in a geometric perspective, identical to that of the original understood as real or true representation. The image is not considered in terms of its resemblance, rather its value is attached to a mathematical and rational equality of relations (*Sophist*, 235c-236c).

There is an effort to establish the fundamental possibility of founding a relation between the image and the original, and to save the notion of image itself. There is an impossibility of image in the absence of any model it resembles, and a disappearance on the other hand of the copy itself if it loses its character of *eikon*, by being a double and thus a moment of ontological forgery. By safeguarding the possibility of the relation of conformity to the model, there can be a difference between copies which are not *phantasmata* or deceptive *simulacra*, very much as in the contrast between true *logos* and the false. The transformation in the notion of image saves the iconic relation and puts in place the foundation of the mimetic.

In Deleuze's *Difference and Repetition* there is a programmatic and agonistic relation to the work of Plato, or what might also be termed as an insistence on contending with Platonism which is for Deleuze the necessary modern situation having as its most immediate consequence the destruction of the model, and the affirmation of simulacra. The programmatic aspect of this work is found in the outline of the eight postulates of the dogmatic image of thought identified by Deleuze, his reading of Nietzsche's teaching on the eternal return, and the tense engagement with the work of Plato because the task of modern philosophy has been defined as the overturning of Plato.

The eight postulates are listed in chapter three, entitled 'The Image of Thought'. The main proposition advanced by Deleuze is that 'to think is to create – there is no other creation – but to create is first of all to engender "thinking" in thought'.[41]

What has prevented this is dogmatic postulates, of which the first is the postulate of the principle, the presumption that is for Deleuze dogmatic, moral and orthodox, the presumption that there is a natural faculty for thought which is endowed with an affinity for truth, of a good-will on the part of the thinker, and an upright nature on the part of thought. This is the general presupposition of philosophy which Nietzsche questions under the rubric 'morality'.

The second postulate is the postulate of the ideal, or common sense. This implies the concordance of faculties and their distribution as effectively guaranteeing this concord. Behind this is the fundamental model which in effect dominates characterisations of thinking, and the model is that of 'recognition'. This means that there is a harmonious exercise of all the faculties upon a supposed object, and the same object may be seen, touched, remembered, imagined or conceived. The recognition is a subjective collaboration of the faculties for 'everybody'. Common-sense is a *concordia facultatum*.

From this the third postulate is also given, the postulate of the model:

The model of recognition is necessarily included in the image of thought, and whether one considers Plato's *Theaetetus*, Descartes' *Meditations*, or Kant's *Critique of Pure Reason*, this model remains sovereign and defines the orientation of the philosophical analysis of what it means to think.[42]

The image of thought is thus universalised in these three postulates to the rational level, to give form to *doxa*. Only the recognised and the recognisable are sanctioned. Nothing really 'new', which is the real affirmation of the Eternal Return, can be created. An ambiguity enters

41 Deleuze, **Difference and Repetition**, p.185.
42 Deleuze, **ibid.**, p.170.

Deleuze's argument here, in that he wonders if the image of thought rather than deriving from the banality of everyday acts of recognition ('this is a table', 'this is a chair'), should not seek its models among 'stranger and more compromising adventures'. The model is also saturated with insignificance and complacency, a thinking that disturbs no-one, and gives itself to monstrous nuptials (the Church, the State), all of which share the transcendental illusion of being eternal objects. In a sense in his comment on this postulate we have one of the dynamic distributions of a thesis as counter-assertion. It is the new, which in other words is difference, that calls forth forces in thought, which are not the forces of recognition, 'but the powers of a completely other model', from an unrecognised and unrecognisable *terra incognita*.[43]

What matters for Deleuze is an intense world of differences, in which the reason behind qualities and the being of the sensible is what he designates as the object of a superior empiricism. It seeks a strange 'reason', of the multiple and difference, in his phrase 'nomadic distributions and crowned anarchies'. Nomadism exhibits how one is distributed in a space, as an errant and 'delirious' distribution, when representation discovers the infinite within itself and sees that it is no longer organic, but orgiastic representation, and it 'rediscovers monstrosity'. The difference and new in affirmation is perforce a 'monster'. Affirmation is creation but it must be affirmed as creating difference, as being difference in itself. It is Eternal Return which effects this true selection, in that it eliminates average forms and uncovers the superior form of everything that is.[44]

Difference cannot be forced by identity, it is affirmation itself. To affirm is light, aerial, it unburdens and discharges. In modern art Deleuze finds this unburdening, and in a highly baroque observation, he sees it as 'the theatre of metamorphosis or permutation'. It is a labyrinth without a thread, and in a cruel, monstrous statement, he says that Ariadne has hung herself.

The work of art leaves the domain of representation to become 'experience', what he nominates as a transcendental empiricism, or science of the sensible. The 'science of the sensible' echoes Baumgarten's definition of the aesthetics, but for Deleuze there is another meaning, namely the apprehension in the sensible that can be sensed, where difference is movement as affect – again a baroque-expressionist, or fundamentally anti-classical request – and phenomena flash their meaning like signs.

Deleuze has already some idea of the *terra incognita*, which flows, because we enter into that schizophrenia which characterises the highest power of thought and opens Being directly to difference, despite all the mediations, all the reconciliation of the concept.

The most profound difference in kind is between average forms and extreme forms, the issue is of new values. Valuation is a fiat, not a reflection. In that sense Eternal Recurrence/Return is present in every metamorphosis, contemporaneous with that which it causes to return, and this relates to a world of differences implicated one in the other, to a complicated, properly chaotic and without-identity production of the new. The element of this is the '*dispars*' which stands opposed to the identity of representation. The circle of Eternal Return as difference and repetition is a torturous circle in which 'Sameness' (sic) is said only of that which differs.

Deleuze draws on Gabriel Tarde to indicate that repetition is the differentiator of difference. Eternal Return is a force of affirmation and it affirms everything of the multiple:

> The eternal return is a force of affirmation, but it affirms everything of the multiple, everything of the different, everything of chance except what subordinates them to the One, the Same and the Necessary.[45]

This last point is also the basis of the fourth postulate, namely, the postulate of the element, or of representation, when difference is subordinated to the Same, the Similar, the Analogous, and the Opposed.

The fifth postulate is the postulate of the negative. This involves a complex argument, which deals with the problem of the question and response in philosophy. The problem structure is part of the signs themselves: what is allowed to be grasped in the act of learning. There is, as it were, an 'opening', a 'gap', an 'ontological fold'. Being is also non-Being, but not the being of the negative; rather it is the being of the problematic, the being of the problem and the question, which should be designated by the typographical mark, '?-being'.

The sixth postulate is that of logical function, or the proposition. Here designation is taken to be the locus of truth, and sense is no more than the neutralised doubling or the infinite doubling of the proposition.

The seventh postulate is that of modality, or solutions, which sees problems being materially traced from propositions and not from the encounters of sense, or being formally defined as the possibility of their being solved. The eighth postulate is the postulate of the end, or result, the postulate of knowledge, that is the subordination of learning to knowledge, and of culture to method.

The postulates need not be spoken, they function all the more effectively in silence, in the presupposition with regard to essence as well as examples. 'Together they form the dogmatic image of thought'. They crush thought under an image which is that of the Same and the Similar in representation, but profoundly betrays what it means to think and alienates the two powers of difference and repetition, of philosophical commencement and recommencement.

The task of overturning this image of knowledge requires the overturning of Platonism. Although the overturning of Platonism may conserve many of its characteristic Deleuze remarks this is not only inevitable but desirable: 'It is true that Platonism already represents the subordi-

43 Deleuze, **ibid.**, p.172.
44 Deleuze, **ibid.**, p.66.
45 Deleuze, **ibid.**, p.141.

[1]

[2]

1 MVRDV, model of balcony dwellings in Zoetermeer, 1997.
2 MVRDV, working model of double house in Utrecht, 1995-97. Rear facade.

nation of difference to the powers of the One, the Analogous, the Similar, and even the Negative'. Nevertheless Deleuze says that with Plato the issue is still in doubt, but that it is rather like an animal being tamed, whose final resistant movements bear witness to a nature soon to be lost: 'the Heraclitean world still growls in Platonism'.[46] The idea has not yet chosen to relate to the identity of a concept in general. The labyrinth or chaos is untangled, but without thread or the assistance of a thread.

The dialectic of difference has its own method, that of division, a capricious, incoherent procedure which jumps from one singularity to another, by contrast with the supposed identity of a concept. For Deleuze it is the dialectical procedure which gathers power in favour of a genuine philosophy of difference. This is not about the dividing of genus into species, as in Aristotle. It is essentially a method of selection. It is true to say that the selection in Eternal Return is what overturns Platonism. The meaning and goal of division is the selection among rivals and claimants, clear in the example of the *Statesman* where the statesman is defined as the one who knows the pastoral care of men, and in the *Phaedrus*, where the question is of defining the good madness and the true lover, as many claimants cry: 'I am love, I am the lover'.

The question is of authenticating and not, as in Aristotle, of identifying. The one problem which recurs throughout Plato's philosophy is the problem of measuring rivals and selecting claimants. This problem of selecting between things and their simulacra within a pseudo-genus or a large species presides over his classification of the arts and sciences. The method of division depends on the introduction of myth. This is evident in the *Phaedrus*, where the myth and contemplating it determines who are the rightful claimants. In the *Sophist* there is no myth, because the method is used paradoxically to isolate the false claimant *par excellence*, the sophist.

Division integrates myth into dialectic. The *Phaedrus* establishes that there is a model of partial circulation which appears as a suitable ground on which to measure the rival claimants. This ground appears as the Idea, such as are contemplated by the souls above the celestial vault. The relation to ground is consequential. It is indicated in participation. Only Justice is just, and those who are just possess the quality of justice in the second place, or in simulacral fashion.

The idea or ground is in first place, the claimant in second: necessarily calling for a ground, it is the nature of every phenomenon. There is the ground Justice, the quality of justice, and the claimants: thus the Neo-Platonic triad: the Imparticipable, the Participated, and the Participants.

The aim, as the Neo-Platonists saw, of division, was the establishment of a serial dialectic. The point about the Sophist is that he is never grounded, but contradicts everything, including himself. But the oracle speaks, and this must then be questioned. Plato proceeds by problems, this is what defines the dialectic. By such means one attains the pure guiding principle. However, Deleuze reads the procedure of division also in another way.

46 Deleuze, **ibid**., p.71.

Deleuze identifies four figures of the Platonic dialectic: the selection of difference, the installation of a mythic circle, the establishment of a foundation, and the position of a question-problem complex. Further, and this is hardly supposed by the *Cratylus* which Deleuze does not discuss, he says that Plato gave the establishment of difference as the supreme goal of dialectic, adding:

> …difference does not lie between things and simulacra, models and copies. Things are simulacra themselves, simulacra are the superior forms and the difficulty facing everything is to become its own simulacra, to attain the status of a sign in the coherence of eternal return. Plato opposed eternal return to chaos, as though chaos were a contradictory state which must be subject to order or law from outside, as it is when the Demiurge subjugates a rebellious matter.

For Deleuze the overcoming of Platonism is contained in what modern art literally indicates to philosophy: a path leading to the abandonment of representation. It is not enough, he contends, to multiply perspectives in order to establish perspectivism. To every perspective or point of view there has to be an autonomous work with its own self-sufficient sense. The totality of circles and series is an ungrounded chaos. The example he gives is *Finnegans Wake*, which is of necessity a problematic work, where the object read is dissolved into divergent series defined by esoteric words, and the identity of the reading subject is dissolved into decentred circles of possible multiple readings.

> Everything has become simulacrum, for by simulacrum we should not understand a simple imitation but rather the act by which the very idea of a model or a privileged position is challenged and overturned.[47]

The simulacrum is the instance which includes difference in itself, and this is the self-engendering of the creative which for Deleuze is the affirmation of how divergent series are played on, at least two, and where all resemblance is abolished so that one can no longer point to the existence of an original and a copy. This is the lived reality of a sub-representative domain. The pure presence granted by the simulacrum has the disparate as the unit of measure, always a difference of difference as its immediate element.

It is now possible to turn to the situation of contemporary art and architec-

   47 Deleuze, **ibid**., p.82.

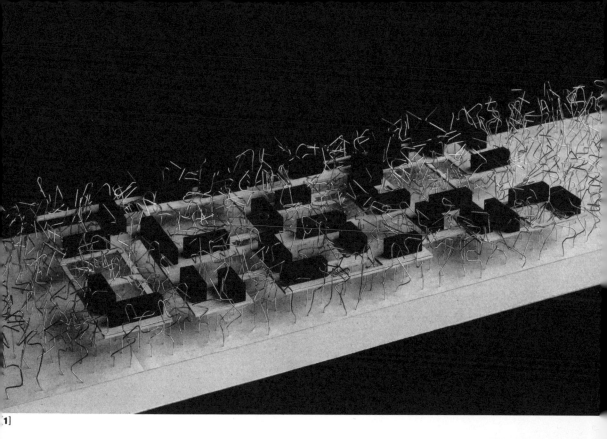

1]

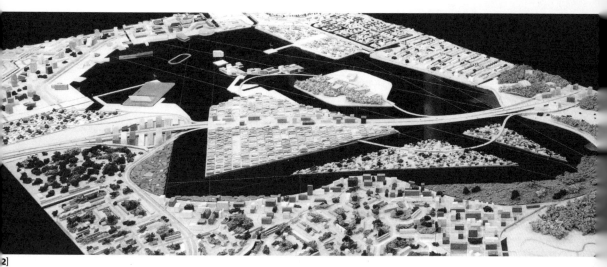

2]

1 MVRDV, model of country estates in
Waddinxveen, variant 2: Skywalk, 1997.
2 MVRDV, model of Weerwater City,
Almere 2015, town planning study, 1996.

[1]

[2]

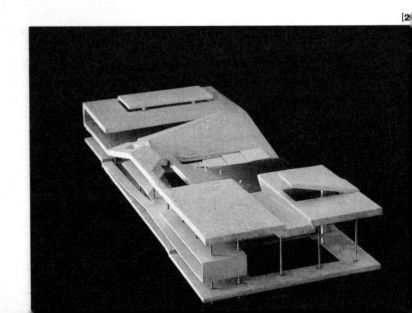

1 MVRDV, concept model of Leidscheveen town centre, 1997.
2 MVRDV, model of Sloterpark swimming pool, 1994.

ture, to see how the path indicated to philosophy has been described, and against the normal chronological ordering it will be fruitful to then return to consider how the different discussions on the model and image have eventuated in different kinds of material embodiment.

Nicolò Sardo, in his work *La Figurazione Plastica dell'architettura*,[48] and Karen Moon, in her work on the model, outline much of the tendencies and activities of contemporary architecture which respond to the problematics discussed above.[49] The model is characterised as the materialising of a concept in the maker's mind. On this account models are closer to reality and more comprehensible than computer images. They convey a range of information about a project and exhibit versatility.

Models can be seen as the exact miniaturising of the energetic representations of the visual and spatial concepts of architects. They communicate messages, and also the image of an architect and how his or her work is to be seen. The 'image' of the architect has increasingly become the 'content' of the building. Models also have limitations because of the reduced scale; interior spaces cannot be explored as freely as with dimensional simulation, film, or video. They are not a convenient way to communicate specifications. They cannot travel easily.

The model is then taken as an element in an architectural process, but which also has an independent existence as an object. As will be indicated in the discussion of Eisenman below, the model, however, is not a miniature building. The model is an idea, and an object; it is about the project but also about itself. Moon cites Michael Graves' observation that once an idea has been modelled or represented, the made object begins to have a life of its own. The model then relates to but is beyond the original conception. The tension in the making of the object, in one scale, is that it becomes an end in itself rather than a process.

There are many views often diametrically opposed about the model: that it is an idea in itself and an idea about objects; that it is an idea about ideas rather than an idea about architecture. In the latter claim is the further view that buildings are the 'physical embodiment', while drawings and models represent the idea. In the former view it has led the discussion towards treating models as sculpture. As indicated later, this is of some concern to Langer in her aesthetic theory of architecture and space. Hadid presented one of her models as a free-standing sculpture at Max Protech's 1999 'Architectural Imagination'.

Moon outlines the increased interest from the 1970s in models, and the attachment of architects to the idea of the model as preserving the unsullied idea. Increasingly they could be seen as creation without responsibility, small works used as a laboratory for stylistic refinements. Product design, as with Michael Graves, could be an alternative format for modelling architectural ideas.

The main import of Moon's arguments is that models in the contemporary practice are created by architects to ensure the validity of their designs and to test technical performance.

48 Nicolò Sardo, see note 18.
49 Karen Moon, **Modelling Messages: The Architect and the Model** (Monacelli Press, 2005).

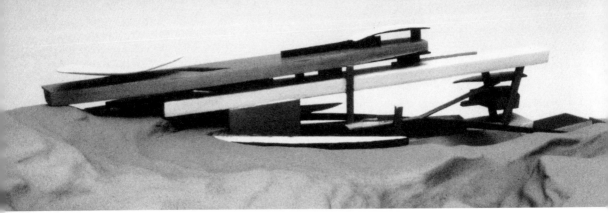

[1]

[2]

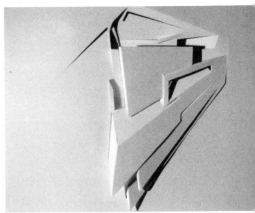

[3]

1 Zaha Hadid, model for The Peak (Leisure Club) Competition, Hong Kong, 1982. Side elevation.
2 Zaha Hadid, study model of extension to the Reina Sofia Museum, Madrid, 1999.
3 Zaha Hadid, exterior perspective relief model for the National Centre of Contemporary Arts, Rome, 1999.

Innovative features require evaluation, especially of costs. This is a favourite trope of Alberti. Nevertheless the guarding of intention and the preserving of original design was of great significance; one sees this, as discussed below, in the tremendous story of Michelangelo and his models for St. Peter's.

Models are also instruments, acts of communication with clients and others. They inform, translate, and argue: they also are a constitutive contributor to the dialogue between design and construction teams. From Vasari's comments on Brunelleschi we will see later how central the use of models became for pragmatic on-site communication. Not everyone understood drawings, and a large and exact model often communicated necessary information.

Moon suggests, and this is also borne out by the research of Sardo, that the 16th century sees the explosion of the model, which became pivotal in the Baroque period, with Neo-Classicism seeing the decline of the model, such that by the end of the 19th century they were seen as an expensive luxury. Moon dates the move away from the Beaux-Arts fascination with virtuoso drawing at the expense of three-dimensional study, and the loss of capacity to think in the solid, to the 1920s.

With the building of skyscrapers new forms for communication were needed, as conventional presentation of elevation, section and plan could mislead the uninitiated. This has led to the thinking that models are finished, presentation style-models made for the client or building committee. For the Kröller-Müller house in Wassenaar, Mies van der Rohe constructed a canvas stretched over a wooden frame. Saarinen made a replica of access stairways to the St. Louis Gateway Arch to see if the lengthening of each successive step would pose a problem for walking. Pei made a diagrammatic model of the Louvre extension from cables. Thus, one could have full-sized models that simulated the design, 'mock-ups' constructed with actual building material.

Small models are used at the beginning of the process to capture essential impressions. They are used for developing formal ideas, exploring massing possibilities, investigating a concept. They facilitate rapid fabrication, and broad appraisal of a project idea. However, as a representation is reduced in scale, design details must be sacrificed. All model making is an abstraction, large or small. The model is a dynamic translation system, converting abstraction into reality. It may be indeed, as Levi-Strauss once remarked, that the power of the small model lies in the way it makes up for a lack of sensual dimensions by an increase in intellectual dimensions.

In a short interview granted in 1981, the architect Peter Eisenman turned to discuss the relation of the model to his work in architecture, providing some trenchant definitions of the model and its significance within his view of architecture. He initially emphasised that his main concern was to separate the sign from the substance of architecture. By substance of architecture he meant the traditional idea of the built building. Such a built building was thought to be symbolic of man or 'mimetic of his condition'.[50]

50 This discussion on Peter Eisenman draws on the following research: Eisenman interviews and writings, the research of Arie Graafland, and the work of Luca Galofaro. For Eisenman at this date, see the following: A. Graafland, **Esthetisch Vertoog en Ontwerp** (Nijmegen: SUN, 1986), where Eisenman is defined as a 'transfunctionalist': 'House X van Eisenman is niet post-modern maar transfunctionalistisch' (p.15); and the further work edited by Graafland (with contributions from Kenneth Frampton, Jeff Kipnis, Jacques Derrida, Peter Eisenman), **Recent Projects** (Nijmegen: SUN, 1989). This publication includes a bibliography of

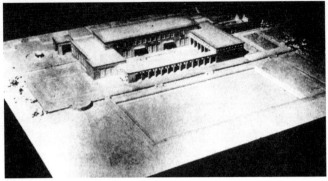

[1]

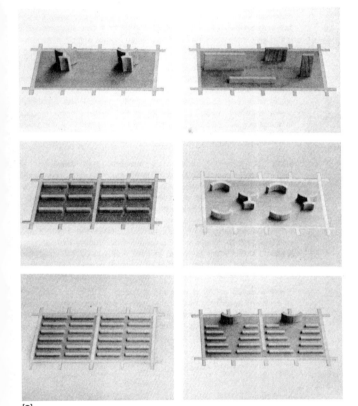

[2]

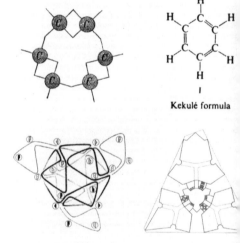

Kekulé formula

[3]

1 Mies van der Rohe, design model for
Kröller-Müller House, 1912.
2 Study models of architectural variations,
maintaining the same density. Work by
students under Mies van der Rohe at the
Illinois Institute of Technology.
3 [Top left] model of benzene ring (after
August Kekulé); [top right] modern symbolic
notation for the benzene ring; [bottom left]
Rudolf von Laban, choreutic shapes performed by the body; [bottom right] Glass
Skyscraper project, 1922, Berlin, plan.
4 I.M. Pei, architect with the model for Le
Grand Louvre, Paris, 1983-89.
5 Eero Saarinen, Massachusetts Institute of
Technology, Cambridge, Mass., 1950-55.
Design sketch of auditorium and chapel.

[4]

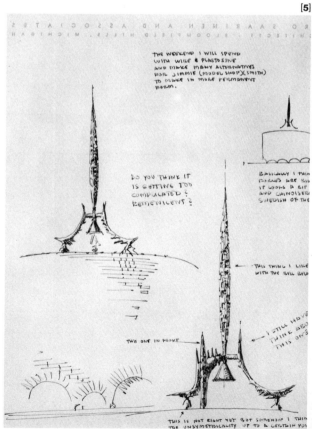

[5]

Identifying an important shift in his own work, he describes it as the shift from the built artefact, as the mark of a traditional sign, to the building as a sign about itself. It was in his first houses that he locates the questioning about the nature of the sign in architecture and about the sign itself:

> The first house was built like a model airplane – the connections between column and beams were actually sanded down and glued together. House II was built to look like a model (often when a photograph of House II is printed in a magazine, it is mistitled a 'model photograph'. Thus while House I was built like a model, House II actually looked like a model.[51]

What he learnt from his initial investigation was that the architectural sign is not like a linguistic sign, since the architectural sign also has substance and sensuous properties. In a pithy observation Eisenman concludes that fundamentally architecture is involved with sensuous properties 'rather than merely with the relationship of signs'.

Eisenman has de-signed architecture at one stroke, introducing a linguistic model which he then radically materialises. The model which he introduces itself emerges out of the reflexive and self-referential practices that mark the possibility for a new research in the discipline of architecture in a post-anthropocentric period where the instrumentalising of optics and transformative media suggest a more complex and dialectical design process.

His first two houses then become a questioning and theoretical act; they question the nature of the sign and the capacity of the sign to be self-referential. The next two houses, he claims, questioned the relationship of the self-referential sign to the substance and poetics of the sign, and finally the last two houses posed the problem of representations in terms of the idea of scale, which ultimately led to the idea of the model.

Eisenman's idea of the model can be, he intimates, understood in two ways. One would be as a representation of ideas (as opposed to buildings); here he identifies the example of Aldo Rossi, whom he sees as creating drawings that are not about architecture to be built, that are not even architectural drawings, but rather drawings of architectural ideas. The second way Eisenman understands the model, is the model as an idea in itself. By this he means an object such as in the case of House x model: 'It is not a representation of anything.'[52]

Before House x he thought of models as notational references, as in the case of House II model where the references were colour coded, adding that the only way you could understand the structure of House II was 'through the model', since you could not experience the notations explicitly in the built object itself.

The motivation behind the development of the axonometric model in House x was that the model could not be appropriated in a conventional way if it was regarded as the reality. What Eisenman wants to highlight is the distinction between a model and a drawing. In the case of House II, the model was made out of Plexiglas and so in the model elements could come apart and be seen, whereas when certain forms overlay each other in a drawing they become confusing. Not only is there a better visibility granted through the model in comparison to drawing, but there was an important mobilisation, which simply stated is the claim that the drawing has a fixed point of view, while you can walk around the model.

Less simply, Eisenman then suggests that the reality of the model could only be seen from a fixed viewpoint, and not from the actual three-dimensional experience. If you approached the titled model and moved around it, it seemed like a distortion. Any displacement from the fixed viewpoint at once revealed the falsity of the model and this particular model was not about the house at all, it was 'about the nature of another kind of object and another kind of reality'.

Eisenman insists that in the model of House X the monocular view at 45° is the only way of seeing the reality which the model possesses. You are forced into this view, which only a camera can achieve, and with the photograph (in this case, the ultimate reality) it is transformed from a model into a two-dimensional representation.

Eisenman insists that this has nothing to do with the idea of decomposition. Rather it is a final distancing of subject and object. He realised as he worked on House X that a model could be about something other than the representation of reality. It could be the reality itself and at the same time a distortion of that reality. The powerful disjunction introduced by Eisenman is the insistence that the physical presence of the model could in its physical presence have 'nothing to do with the idea of its presence'. The axonometric model fixes the viewpoint of the viewer, simply because of its smaller scale with respect to the individual who walks around it, it challenges the traditional idea of possessing the model as an object. Possession is only possible from a particular viewpoint.

Here, the understanding of the model has shifted; it is in fact no longer a model, but must be understood as a drawing. In his axonometric model he investigates the nature of the model, the nature of scale, and the relationship of these factors to the individual, the viewer, who can no longer possess it.

Eisenman adds that there are three variations in his oeuvre on this idea: House X, the project

articles and books by Eisenman, from 1963 to 1988, and a secondary literature of articles in books, catalogues and periodicals from 1980-1988. This can be updated from the text of Luca Galofaro, **Digital Eisenman** (translated by Lucinda Byatt from the original Italian published in Turin in 1999, **Eisenman Digitale**). The relation with Piranesi depends on the reading of Manfredo Tafuri, **La sfera e il labirintho** (Turin, 1980). Galofaro's publication contains the essay 'Visions Unfolding: Architecture in the Age of Electronic Media', by Peter Eisenman, and is crucial for the relation to the notion of 'the electronic paradigm', on which he writes; Galofaro, **op. cit.**, pp.84-89. Galofaro worked in Eisenman's office in 1996-7 inclusive. The most recent publication of Peter Eisenman, his thesis from 1963 (published by Lars Müller), has been reviewed by Graafland in **Footprint**, the Journal of the Delft School of Design, 2007; see: www. footprint.org. See also: Greg Lynn, 'Aronoff Center', in **Domus**, no.788, December 1998. See also: M. Christine Boyer, **Cybercities** (Princeton: Princeton Architectural Press, 1996).
51 'A Poetics of the Model: Eisenman's Doubt', interview between Peter Eisenman, David Shapiro and Lindsay Stamm, March 8, 1981, **Idea as Model**, IAUS Catalogue 3 (New York: Rizzoli International, 1981), pp.121-125.
52 Idem.

for Cannaregio, and House El Even Odd. What is crucial in following the
further comments of Eisenman is to understand how the change of scale in the
different projects becomes reflexive.

The project for Cannaregio took House IIa and built it as three differently
scaled objects. One of the objects is about four feet high, it sits in the square and
is the model of a house. You can look at it and think: 'well, that is not a house, it
is the model of House IIa'. Then you take the same object and put it in House
IIa, which sits inside what seems to be another, real-life House IIa.

Decisively for Eisenman when you put the model of House IIa inside, it is
no longer a model, because once you monumentalise, it becomes the object
itself. The larger object memorialises the smaller one. Once memorialised, the
smaller object inside the larger one is no longer a model. What has taken place is
that the original four-foot high object which was a model of something has been
transformed into the real thing. As a result, the larger house, the one at anthropomorphic scale, no longer functions as a house.

Then there is a third object which is larger than the other two, which is
larger than reality, larger than an anthropomorphic necessity. The largest one
contains the middle-sized one and the little one, which completes the reflexive
cycle. It becomes a museum of all these things. Because of the change in scale all
three take on different names, and different meanings, not in relationship to the
individual but to their own change in scale – they become reflexive.

This emphasis by Eisenman is itself a reflection on a shift identified for
modern sculpture in its shift from representation to abstraction, which is the
shift from scale-specific to scale non-specific. That is to say, the reflexivity that
Eisenman notes for his models is equivalent to the self-referentiality of the scale
in the non-specific abstraction of modern sculpture, which is also a result of
sculpture ceasing to be anthropomorphic. Whereas in architecture it had been
the case that, being scale-specific, the model could always be related to its own
level, as it was evidently smaller than the scale of human usage.

Eisenman points to the work of Aldo Rossi to reinforce his point, where the
issue of scale is very clear. Rossi's work points to a disassociation between the
scale of the city on the outside and the scale of the individual and the living cell
on the inside; the example being the window in the Gallatrese which is too large
for the interior room, but is the right scale for the city. In Rossi's architecture,
the reference is to the displacement between interiority and exteriority, and not
to the individual scale. It is this disassociation which Eisenman understands as
self-referential. It is this self-referentiality he identifies for the sculpture for
example of Brancusi and Sol LeWitt, and which is active in the principle of his
own projects as analysed by the architect himself.

Another consequence following on the reflexive is that the objects suggest a
whole series of ideas which have nothing to do with the size of man in relationship to the object (whether it is bigger than man, the right size, or smaller).

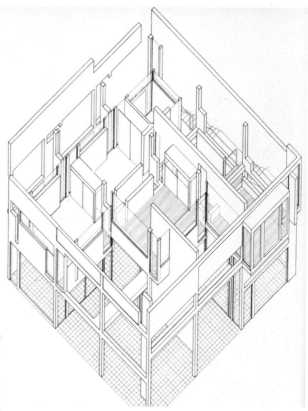

[1]

[2]

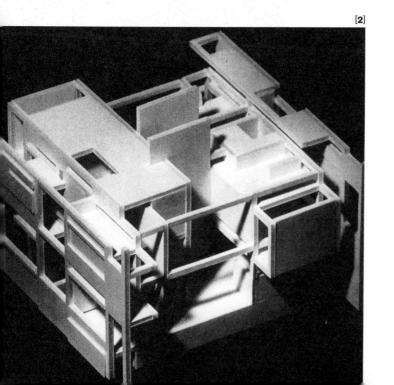

1 Peter Eisenman, House II, 1969-1970.
Axonometric perspective.
2 Peter Eisenman, House IV, 1971. Study
model.

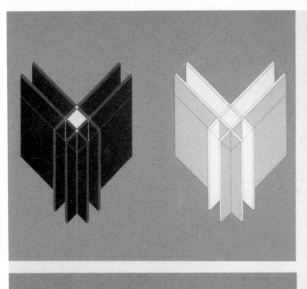
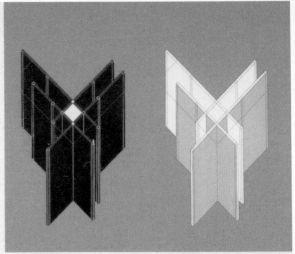
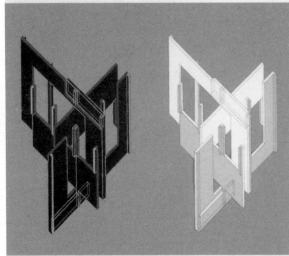

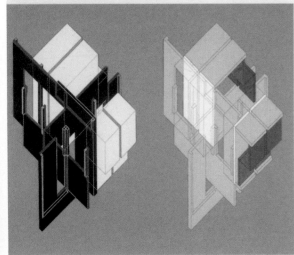

[1]

[2]

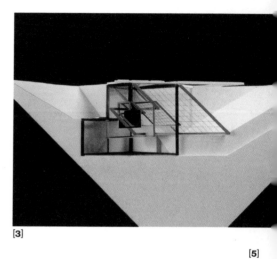

[3]

[5]

4]

Peter Eisenman, House VI, Cornwall,
Connecticut, 1972-75. Axonometric
diagrams and image.
  Peter Eisenman, House X, Bloomfield,
Michigan. Axonometric model.
  Peter Eisenman, House El Even Odd.
View of sectional model.
  Aldo Rossi, model of design for Monte
Amiata in Naples, Italy, 1988.
  Aldo Rossi, model and design sketch of
Yatai of Pinokkio, Mobile installation for
Japan Design Expo '89, Nagoya, Japan.

In the House El Even Odd, one begins with what appears to be an axonometric model which has itself become the reality. This reality is then transformed; it becomes an axonometric drawing and simultaneously a plan of itself, and so 'the supposed model of House El Even Odd is not the model at all; again it has become another reality'. This is almost a double-take in Eisenman's account, because he insists that with House El Even Odd, when you make a plan of it, it looks like an axonometric, and when you project it on an axonometric, it looks like a plan. There is then a complete reversal, and a dislocation that has nothing to do with the object itself, because as he emphasises, a plan is not a reality, but merely a projection of reality.

The axonometric model distorts and opens up an investigation into representation. It is no longer just a means of representation. It becomes an idea in itself, and an idea about objects, rather than just a manner by which objects may be distanced from the subject.

If, with respect to scale and the disjunctive experience that Eisenman insists on, there is a loss of relationship to the normative of the human scale, then in respect to idealisation the question of perspective and distance has also undergone a profound shift. Eisenman situates this historically, saying that if one looks at Palladio's architecture, it can be seen as a re-reading of the notion of perspective put forward by Brunelleschi and Bramante. Perspective, a mode of representation, changed the relationship of the viewer to the object, and the way the viewer moved in relation to the object became very important. In Eisenman's terse summary of complex issues he views Palladio as forcing the object to have distance from the subject within the framework of perspective, by flattening out the object, by distorting the actual perspective, by making it more like a drawing, more representational.

Relationships are less hierarchical in terms of subject and object in a world which is no longer anthropocentric. Then viewing the world via the axonometric as a standards means of presenting the object, which has nothing to do with the way man views it, opens up the limits of the discipline of architecture to further study, as Palladio did.

Palladio is interpreted in this re-reading, and Eisenman's own work in its highly charged didactic and processual self-consciousness, inserts itself in a tradition as a form of sub-version, where the shift of the relation of text and commentary allows a transgressive and blind feature of the search for image to guide his working procedures.

The tools of work are themselves caught up in the relativisation; they themselves, as in the case of the axonometric, are means of opening up the discipline. Thus the break with the traditional is explicit in the Cannaregio project; it attempted an architecture that was scale non-specific. Here the movement towards the sculptural in the modernist account that Eisenman argues for is also a movement towards the limit, and indeed the question of the limit for movement. The limits are also part of the traditional questions for any architecture, notions which have defined an 'in quotes' architecture. These notions primarily include shelter, use and construction.

Again, the question of method and content become equally ambivalent, and how to account for the experience of the model as opposed to a building. Eisenman reflects on his own practice and his houses. The first diagrams yielded, as in chess, a series of other moves, which eventually led to a conclusion or a product. By House VI this had changed, and paradoxically Eisenman claims that House VI is a sequence of diagrams which are non-sequential, which merely describe sign and substance. For in reality the house object, the physical subject of the house, is like a film, a series of stills that run together. However, to understand the house you have to literally run it backwards, to a series of still images. The house is not to be understood by standing in it; it is sensed as a result of a process.

In the beginning of the discussion of the model with Eisenman, one is already placed in the snare of doubts that accompany the creative process itself. Eisenman's method and procedure have recently been the subject of a short insider account by Luca Galofaro, where one has a close-up view of the way models are used in the Eisenman office as both a creative and cognitive strategy.

The use of models is not mechanical but invested with a complexity that Galofaro notes 'can be compared with the sphere of the philosophy of science'. He distinguishes the use of three models in the office of Eisenman: plastic models, diagrammatic models and computer models. Diagrammatic and study models are developed simultaneously. The models are heuristic in that they afford the possibility of seeing in advance what the building will look like, and the models, diagrams and computer models intercommunicate during the design process. It is the process of intercommunication during the design task that elaborates in the course of the design process figurative and conceptual possibilities. Talking is one of the most testing tools for designing. Good discourse designs as it speaks.

Instruments of research include writing and publication, through the overlapping which the model clarifies there is also the reflexive activity that, functioning like a hypertext, animates the earlier processes. This highly dynamic process within the project takes a view of the process as an open totality within time itself. It is this temporal dimension that necessarily includes all the aspects of the project, the how it happens in time, which relativises the various ways in which the procedures as initially set out become inter-connective.

It is a feature which one can see taken to its logical conclusion in the 'morphic resonance' of Kas Oosterhuis' notion of the swarm in the hyperbody, except that Eisenman's research remains at a more formal level, and does not include as in the case of Oosterhuis a reference to the direct democracy of the research by design itself, probably guided by another model, namely the Polder model.[53]

---

53 Kas Oosterhuis, **Hyperbodies, Towards an E-motive Architecture** (Basle: Birkhäuser, 2003). This work, which is a manifesto, advances the picture of contemporary architecture as processes running in real time. The architect is the designer of intelligent vehicles, and architecture itself become the model-maker, creating prototypes for fluid structures. Oosterhuis develops a process philosophy which still stays attached to the idea of a productive paradigm.

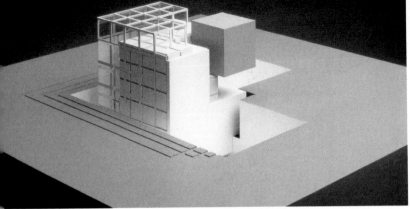

[1]

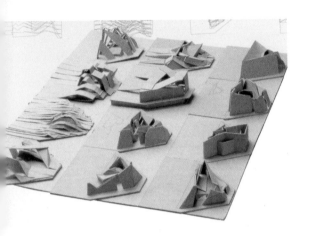

[2]

[3]

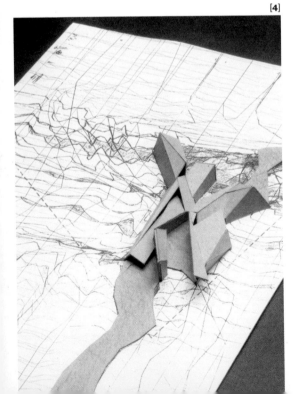

[4]

1 Peter Eisenman, model for Fin d'Ou T Hou S, 1983.
2 Peter Eisenman, study models for Churc of the Year 2000, Rome, Italy, 1996.
3 Peter Eisenman, site and landscape mo for Church of the Year 2000, Rome, Italy, 1996.
4 Peter Eisenman, study model for Biblio-thèque de L'IHUEI, Geneva, Switzerland, 1996-7.

The reflexive commitment itself interacts and intervenes, also creating new instruments. Reflection on modernity leads to the reinvention of a system in which an instrument plays a part in production and where information becomes a system capable of generating possible spaces. The research team uses various means to have the design process interpret the object to be constructed.

Because Eisenman does not see a difference between the model and the building other than that the model is not lived in, the plastic model already is a means that allows the building to be visualised. Each phase of the design process is accompanied by this instrument of representation, which interacts with other models. With respect to diagrammatic models the project does not strictly depend on iconic representations.

What Galofaro points out, and which makes further sense of the discussion of the problem of overlapping and scale, is that there is an examination of typological systems; the latter are then overlapped with deformation diagrams, a good example being the project for the church in Rome where the traditional architectonic diagram, two parallel bars and the void between them, is over-layered by the diagrams of liquid crystals which offer deformations that produce deformations capable of modelling space.

In the case of the architecture it is the critical which acts as the instrument of deformation, and the activation of the consequences of a non-hierarchical relation of subject and object and a de-privileging of the centrality of the human, release design possibilities that are generated through the instruments and technologies of seeing.

Eisenman can also be seen as engaged with the work of Piranesi. As Harbison has recently argued, Piranesi's work changes the relation of part to whole, and also invests in the subjectivity of the view, which is a concrete physical inclusion in the work itself. This inclusion in the frame is part of the anti-Rococo bias in Piranesi, and demands of the viewer an intensification of sensation. Harbison reads this as more akin to Bernini, except that the swoon and derangement inculcated in the experience is part of the strategy of Piranesi, to create ruins of horror which have become voluminous. The spaces are immensely dysfunctional and require an active participation of the viewer to experience and disentangle. At times the legibility is an experience of shock and dislocation.[54]

Unlike the generalised views of earlier periods, Piranesi provides close-ups in which the content and meaning of the work is submerged in the monumental gloom and precise archaeological detail. Part and whole are in an active tension, fragments are viewed scenically, and as in the 'black box' of the theatre, the illusion for the view is inevitably a surrender to the illusion *tout court*.

For Benjamin, in the *Trauerspiel* the ruin is the baroque metaphor *par excellence*, because the allegorical physiognomy of natural-history, which is put on stage in the *Trauerspiel*, is present in

54 Robert Harbison, **Reflections on Baroque** (London: Reaktion Books, 2002)

reality in the form of the ruin. History in the ruin has physically merged into the setting. This is the mask of decay which history wears, not a suggestion of eternal life. For Benjamin 'allegories are in the realm of thoughts what ruins are in the realm of things'. Borinski traced the picturesque of the ruin to the practice of placing the Birth of Christ and the Adoration in the ruins of an antique temple, e.g. Ghirlandaio (Florence, Accademia). Benjamin adds however, that what is significant is that what lies in ruins there is far more than the reminiscence of antiquity; rather, it is the highly significant fragment, the remnant, which is in fact the finest material in baroque creation. There is a baroque practice of piling up fragments, without any strict idea of a goal, and in the unremitting expectation of a miracle to take the repetition of stereotypes as a process of intensification. A new whole is constructed out of the legacy of antiquity, 'for the perfect vision of the new phenomenon was the ruin'.[55]

The diagrams show a building which is emergent in the way of bonding valencies or molecular modelling in crystals. The issue of symmetry in the crystal at the iconic level is instead released into what can be called an emergent geometry at the edge of chaos; this is where the complexity occurs, and where indeed the design process is temporally saturated.

Effectively the overlapping through the diagrammatic is superimposed on the site, guided towards the object, and then transformed into a 3D relation of solids and voids within the complex, emergent, interstitial spaces, programme is assigned.

This overlapping respects the in-between of the interstitial spaces that emerge, as in this case of the behaviour of the liquid crystals and the chosen architectonic diagram, and as Galofaro notes, the building is born through reciprocal influence and elaboration.

This 'in-between' is also a commitment to the view of the design process as highly mobile, open, and experimental. The process is not a series of small steps towards some solution, but each part of the process is itself the emerging of the solution.

An early analysis of the Eisenman project by Arie Graafland gathers up critical consideration of this conceptual commitment, and the commitment of Eisenman to studying the work of accumulation and disruption, layering and folding; how the overlapping of layers and grids results in new spatial techniques that emerge from the instruments of mapping, scaling, superposition, the 'imprinting of movement'.[56]

---

55 Walter Benjamin, **The Origin of German Tragic Drama (Ursprung des deutschen Trauerspiels)**, trans. John Osborne (London: New Left Books, 1977), p.178.
56 Graafland's **Architectural Bodies** (Rotterdam: 010, 1996) is an investigation of the hidden mechanisms which structure the architectural object and give it social relevance. His analysis of the 'social condenser' in understanding how OMA's projects are assembled refers to a design process as deploying a 'paranoid-critical method', as seen in the Downtown Ath-

[1]

2]

[3]

Giambattista Piranesi, etching of a
ew of the Pantheon and its entrance,
25 × 350 mm.
Giambattista Piranesi, etching of a rear
ew of the Pantheon, 190 × 390 mm.
Kas Oosterhuis, model for glass pavilion,
992.

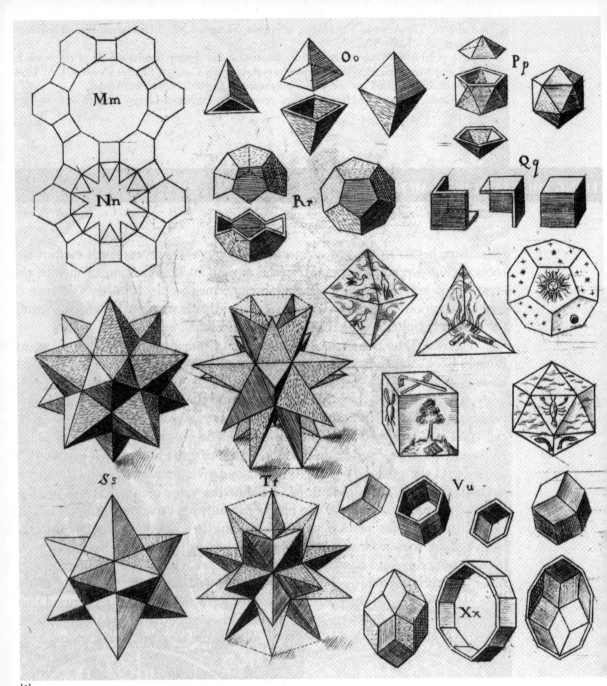

1 Polyhedra from Johannes Kepler's
Harmonica Mundi (Lindz, 1619).

[1]

Graafland's 'Peter Eisenman's Architecture in Absentia' suggests that in considering the designs of Eisenman we may be dealing with what Foucault calls 'situation-objects', by which is understood those visible forms which capture a moment, and which reactivate the not immediately discernible relation between persons. They can be set against figuration-objects, such as cages, dungeons, and the machine. In considering the Eisenman House x Graafland argues that Eisenman reverses the traditional way of designing.

It is to be noted that the 'transformational and linear process of the earlier houses has been repressed'; not a single step is easily predictable or causally related to another. He draws attention to the similarity in working method of Eisenman with that of Bernard Tschumi, and makes the trenchant observation that the designs following House x formulate an architectural problem that probes the limits of what is, and what is no longer architecture.

Architecture is stretched to its limit, and drawing on Derrida and Kristeva, Graafland sees this stretching as a passion for the game of meanings, which erupts in the invention of new forms and contents which are to 'displace the old order'.

There is a transgressive element in which, according to Tschumi, 'architecture seems to survive in its "erotic" capacity when it negates itself'. The question of erotic energy as waste, excess, is a trope of particular significance to Bataille. It also is the inscription of another metaphor within a metaphor, a model within a model, namely the economic theory of Keynes on disequilibrium as the valorised distribution of the erotic as 'excess' escaping from the target of the model of economic rationality, and the premise of utility theory.

Graafland notes some salient points when considering the then-recent designs, among which he counts House x: one being that trust in human rationality is more problematic, because in considering the Romeo and Juliet project for Verona, the design for Parc de la Villette and the Fin d'Ou T Hou S, there are so many arrangements employed that a single reading definitely belongs to the past. Graafland captures the issue of the paradigm shift in the new anarchism by a brief consideration of the 'scaling' problem.[57]

The 'scaling' process, putting aside the human scale, is applied in order to understand three philosophical fields; presence and absence of an object or construction of a formerly hidden presence by means of an absence, recursivity affecting (philosophy of) origin, and self-similarity commenting on representation are three effects not intended before House x.

House x should be considered a turning point, having as its most important aim 'the drastic modification of architectural codes reaching further than modernity' ('het drastisch verzetten van de architectonische codes die verder reiken dan de moderniteit'). The complex introduction of significance as a rhetorical figure for architecture is to make of it a capacity for rhetorical

letic Club. Eisenman cancels the symbolic order in the Biocenter design, and creates discontinuities. As in radical cubist fragmentation, the human body is stripped of unity. Nevertheless the body metaphor is an invisible and abstract process which structures bodily experience. Assemblages belong to the machinic.

57 The remote ancestor of this problem in architecture is Serlio, who creates the 'machine' of the 'orders', turning desire into regulated production. Serlio creates what Mario Carpo calls 'an articulate repertoire (paradigmatic and syntagmatic) of standardised and repeatable architectural components that could be combined in accordance with strict rules and that functioned as semantic signs' (p.49); what can be called 'paper models', thanks to the technology significance, even as absence, away from its traditional substance as symbolising *of the 'human'*. New meanings are constantly invented and situated in the design process. Graafland calls this movement in design for Eisenman 'anti-thetic'.

Remarkably it is in the study of the Biocenter that one can delineate the process and problem of the model in a fascinating way. Here is a project of Eisenman which is itself modelled on a model. Again Graafland can serve as a guide.[58] What is at issue, he states, is how to understand the dynamics, the 'strange intersections' noted by Philip Johnson. The process followed in the design is derived from the DNA model. Of course this is not a literal transcription. Eisenman's research is just that, and is not content to find a historiography or theory about the local and then provide it with cultural content. He focuses on the problem of linearity and discontinuity in history. Eisenman by focusing on the ruptures and the discontinuities is engaged in a tearing apart and separation, and the key to the interpretation of the Biocenter is, as Philip Johnson points out, *'reissen'*. Johnson takes this term in a very literal sense, of 'tearing apart'.

What Graafland's analysis shows is that it is the duplication, translation and transcription within the model of the DNA which is of significance to Eisenman. While one can point to a graphic copying of the four nucleotoids in the plan, the enzymes which split the DNA molecule apart, he does not take the ladder structure of the double helix for his design. It is not the double helix model that has been the starting point for his design, it is rather the three processes of doubling DNA that have acted as the starting point. Thus there is a model based on a model, but it would be better to say a research process which tracks and follows the inner process that is being modelled in bio-chemistry.

Thanks to Galofaro's account we have a close-up witness to the way in which this process proceeds. One can follow the diagrammatic to the point where there are 'possibilities offered in a practical spatial application'. Where the solid is compressed and deformed, so too is the void, there is a dynamic action and reaction. Thus in an analysis of the Library in the Place des Nations in Geneva, the diagrammatic structure follows the operation of the brain, allowing for its highly mobile plasticity. This creates a condition in which there is a possibility for modelling space. These diagrams are super-imposed on the site grid, and

of printing and the imaging of architecture through this process. Mario Carpo in his **L'architettura dell'eta della stampa** (Milan: Jaca Books, 1998), and published in translation by Sarah Benson (MIT, 2001) as **Architecture in the Age of Printing**. The Serlian orders are architectural microdesigns, ready for use, but with some assembly required, what Carpo calls the **prêt-a-porter** line of Renaissance composition. The consequence of the ready reproduction of image has resulted in the post-modernist and x-modernist situation today, in an architecture of screen and surface.

58 The sublime belongs to an intensive realism, and Graafland specifically calls for an architecture that uses perfection and imperfection as conceptual tools, which could create a socius of architectural and revolutionary inscription, because the surface holds the 'other' reality, that society is a **socius** of inscription, where the essential thing is to mark and be marked; however it is a **socius** which is a full body on which all production material and immaterial is recorded. The view of the city on this account is close to Aristotle, as I have argued elsewhere, see note 33.

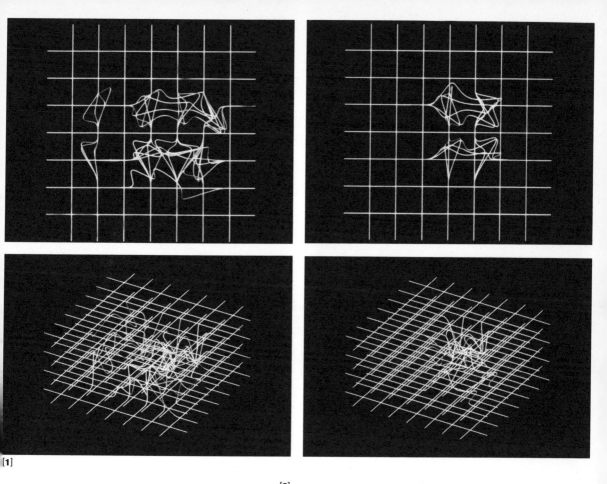

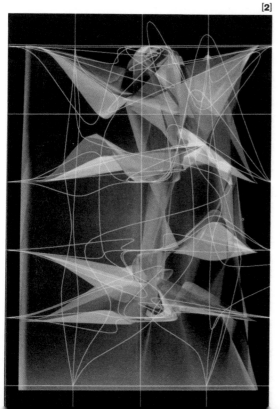

1, 2 Peter Eisenman, Virtual House Competition, 1997. Diagrams of genesis.
3 A conventional ball-and-stick model of the structure of DNA.

Peter Eisenman, Virtual House Competition,
1997. Section of competition model.

according to Galofaro, Eisenman records the different elements and then transforms them into design constraints, incorporating them in the mechanical process that generates the object directly from the site. The new building emerges between the landscape and the objects, putting both conditions out of focus in a single heterogeneous space.

One can follow the sequence precisely, once the conceptual determination is made as to the research object, thus in the case of synaptic activity its randomness as a heterogeneous and self-organised system, dominated by arbitrary combinations, actually creates an evolutionary process. There is a diagram with a superimposition of activity separation frequencies, then a superimposition of the tracings of memory in an emotional state, further superimpositions of tracings and frequencies, and then superimposition of diagrams on the site. The key point is that the diagrams are evolving and develop into a vectoral system which becomes computerised models.

In one sense, the working method of Eisenman seeks to find a way to control the superimpositions, and as in the library project this depends critically on his accepting a graphic display from brain scanning as an analogue to the living process, which is critically a kind of uncertainty. In Galofaro's reading Eisenman uses the computers and models to work simultaneously from inside and outside. The fluidity of the space of the central passage in the Aronoff Center becomes a continuing adventure in space, with the element of surprise throughout, suggesting to Galofaro that there is something reminiscent of Piranesi.

What is probably most clear is what Sedlmayr called the loss of centre. It is this which creates a reading of the '80s architecture as anarchic, if not revolutionary. Eisenman achieves forms through spatial manipulation, not out of projection from bodies or materials. It is this which the computer models help one track.

The virtual is in Eisenman's work the realisation of the actual in time, it is the possibility in the moment of the process, and the models come from other disciplines. The argument for this is that the architecture of diagrams is correlated with the vectoral systems and this is then materialised. The process of materialisation is that the ideas being elaborated become information. Thus mathematics, biology and physics become information and available for translation into architectural concepts.

Graafland's analysis of the Eisenman Biocenter had already shown the complex direction of this research and process. If initially the question had been the relationship of architecture to art, increasingly the process of design itself became autonomous, and models for architecture were no longer from within traditional architectural convention but increasingly derived from other disciplines. Once again the shift in technology has profound implications for architectural practice and discourse.

We can return to consider the virtual and the computer through Eisenman's project of the virtual house. It allows one to capture what it is that Eisenman claims has happened to architecture; the

[1]

[2]

[3]

1 OMA, Casa da Musica, 2001.
Study model.
2 OMA, MAB Tower, Rotterdam, 2004.
Study model.
3 OMA, Almere Urban Redevelopment /
Block 6 model, 2005. North view.

paradigm shift from the 'mechanical paradigm to the electronic one'. Eisenman's article published in *Domus 1992* allows one to chart the movement since the 1980s in terms of fragmentation to that of folds. Characteristically, Eisenman offers a text which is also a programmatic statement, the situation is fraught and instantly polemical, the language that of a skilled rhetorician.[59]

The electronic paradigm offers a 'powerful' challenge to architecture, because it defines reality in terms of media and simulation; it values appearance over existence, what can be seen over what is.

This is not just a clash between intelligibility and the phenomenal, because the seeing which is now privileged is one we can no longer interpret. Media introduces fundamental ambiguities into what and how we see. What the electronic paradigm questions, and what Eisenman says remained unquestioned, is the dominance for architecture of the 'mechanics of vision', equated here with the importation and absorption of perspective by architectural space in the 15th century. In Eisenman's account vision is the particular characteristic of sight that attaches thinking to seeing, the eye to the mind.

This generated the primary discursive terms of architecture, the seeing human subject, monocular and anthropomorphic. The tradition of planimetric projection in architecture allowed the projection and hence the understanding of a three-dimensional space in two dimensions. The sight/mind construct has persisted in architecture as the dominant discourse.[60]

There have been attempts in architecture to overcome 'its rationalising vision'; the notable examples cited include Piranesi, where Eisenman claims Piranesi diffracted the monocular subject by creating perspectival visions with multiple vanishing points. Cubism equally attempted to deflect the relationship between a monocular subject and object, it flattened objects to the edges, and upturned objects, it undermined the stability of the picture plane. The International Style was a normalising version of cubism.

But, in fact there was no shift between subject and object. While the object looked different, it failed to displace the viewing subject. Modern sculpture did effect such a displacement, and such dislocations were fundamental to minimalism; Eisenman cites Robert Morris, Michael Heizer and Robert Smithson. Their achievements are then described as 'a historical project' not taken up by architecture.

Architecture did not question vision, because it remained within the concept of the subject and the four walls. For architecture to take up the question of vision, means for Eisenman not a study of perceptual dynamics; rather, 'vision' can be defined as a way of organising space and elements in space. It is a way of looking, and defines a relationship between subject and object. Typological conditions of architecture provide a means for understanding the position occupied by the subject in relation to any particular typology, rotunda, transept crossing, an axis, an entry. These typologies deploy architecture as a screen for looking at.

59 The article appeared in **Domus 1992**, no.734, 1992, pp.17-21.
60 P. Gregory, **Newscapes: Territories of Complexity** (Basle: Birkhäuser, 2003).

Drawing on the work of Norman Bryson from his article 'The Gaze in the Expanded Field', Eisenman wonders if there can be a looking-back which will offer the possibility of detaching the subject from the rationalisation of space. This requires detachment of space from traditional vision, and a re-inscription that inscribes space in such a way that it has the possibility of looking back at the subject.

How can one conceptualise away from gridded space? In some way architecture is full of inscription, as for example in Baroque and Rococo where the stucco decoration began to obscure the traditional form of functional inscription. Architecture resists excess because of the power of functional inscription.

In what way, Eisenman wonders, could the inscription of an outside text translate into space? Would this inscription be the equivalent of the looking back of the other? Eisenman goes to the text of Deleuze, and suggests that his view of folded space articulates a new relationship between vertical and horizontal, figure and ground, inside and out, as structured and articulated by traditional vision, and that unlike the space of classical vision, the idea of folded space denies framing in favour of a temporal modulation. Rather than planimetric projection, there is a variable curvature. Folding for Eisenman constitutes a move from effective to affective space, and in the affective one must change the relationship of project drawing and real space.[61]

There is no longer a one-to-one correspondence; in an affective environment reason become detached from vision. Reason becomes detached from the environment itself, and this begins to produce an environment that looks back. There is an order that can be perceived, even though it seems to mean nothing. It possesses some sense of 'aura', an ur-logic which is something outside of vision. Because the environment looks back, presents its 'vision', the question of what space means to the viewer is no longer relevant. The perception that there is another order is sufficient to dislocate the knowing subject. It is with the fold that one has a dislocation of the dialectical distinction between figure and ground and in the process it animates a 'smooth space'.

Eisenman interprets Deleuze's 'smooth space' to mean the possibility of overcoming or exceeding the grid. The question of what is *espace quelconque* in Deleuze relates to his theory of nomadism and de-territorialisation. The notion of inhabiting also contains the tension of the being that is 'in-habit', so that the belonging to environment for each organism, requires that the organism escape its territory. This process is for Deleuze a de-territorialisation, of space, a

61 Deleuze, **Le Pli: Leibniz et le baroque** (Paris: Editions de Minuit, 1988).

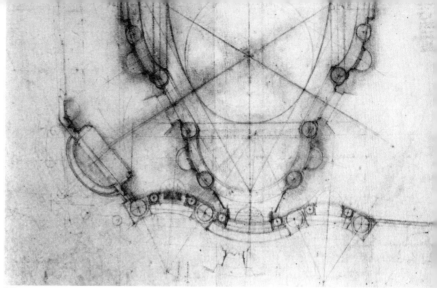

[1]

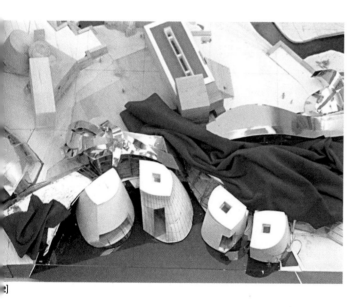

[2]

[3]

1 Francesco Borromini, San Carlo alle
Quattro Fontane, Rome. Sketch plan.
2 Frank Gehry, Lewis Residence, Lyndhurst,
Ohio, 1989-95. Design process model.
3 Fabric folds and twists around an elbow.
Photo: G. Bruyns, 2008.

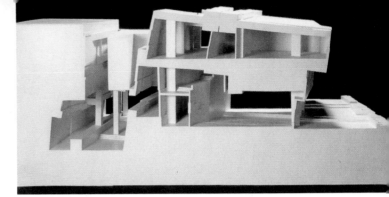

[1]

[2]

[3]

1 Peter Eisenman, Aronoff Centre for Design and Art, Cincinnati, Ohio, 1998-1996. Sectional model.
2, 3 Peter Eisenman, Aronoff Centre for Design and Art, Cincinnati, Ohio, 1988-1996. Exterior.

smooth space, or an *espace quelconque*. This space is variable according to the forces that produce or distribute it, and Deleuze holds that such a smooth space is subject to a distribution which is nomadic, that is, it has no property, enclosure or measure. Persons are arrayed in such a space; where nothing belongs to anyone, there is constant distribution. As noted earlier this is a delirious, wandering space.

One finds in *A Thousand Plateaus* further observations by Deleuze and Guattari, where degrees of deterritorialisation are indicated. Significantly they consider that it becomes most expressive of a single energy which may be termed cosmic. It is the cosmic forces of creation that enact deterritorialisation. Movement is absolute when it is related, then the nomad is placed in a local absolute, an absolute that is manifested locally, in a series of local operations of varying orientations (desert, steppe, ice, sea), to a body considered as multiple and a smooth space that it occupies in the manner of a vortex. But this absolute goes on through what is relative, a relative movement which relates a body considered as one to a striated space through which it moves and which it measures with straight lines. The emergent energy of the cosmic which radiates into image, and is transformed through image, distributes according to no determined causality.

Speaking of the Alteka Tower project, Eisenman notes that it was no longer possible to draw a line that stands for some scale-relationship to another line in the space of the project, as the drawn lines have no longer anything to do with reason. Questions such as what space means are no longer relevant.

Architecture will continue to stand up, deal with gravity, to have 'four walls', but these four walls need no longer be expressive of the mechanical paradigm, rather they could deal with the possibility of other discourses, the other affective senses of sound, touch and of that light lying within the darkness.

In his *Territories of Complexity*, Paolo Gregory observes that the fold as tie, weave, 'between', holds a central place in the architectural research of the 1990s. The thrust of this was a move away from the fragment and de-construction which had been showcased in the 1988 MoMA exhibition to which Tschumi, Koolhaas, Hadid, Eisenman, Libeskind, Gehry, and Coop Himmelb(l)au had been invited.

During the '90s the move was effectively to the 'smooth' space which Eisenman attributed to Deleuze. One can see in projects of Eisenman during this decade his textual elaboration modelling again the practice of design and emerging from that practice. In the competition design for Rebstock Park in Frankfurt (1990) at the very beginning of the decade, fold and field interact with the force field still in the optique of deformation, and the concepts of dislocation and environment from which the human subjects and architecture's traditional commitment to monocular perspective emerge is radically out of joint.

In the Max Reinhardt Haus in Berlin (1992), Gregory says that he 'folds the tower on itself, outlining a Boolean arc that suggests the transfiguration and liquefaction of the form itself,' and later in the urban competition for the Klingelhofer Triangle in Berlin (1995), there is an overlay again of different figured patterns, a clockwork mechanism and a computer chip that become generative of design diagrams and literally create a musical jam session; this is graphic jamming, in which new and unexpected 'events' occur.

The event occurs in the interior of the fold, with the vectors producing continuous deformation, and these spatial transformations required a topological science. One sees in the process itself enormous flexibility, where the directions and vectors are followed and themselves multiply meanings. In a sense, then, virtual wholes manage to sustain different kind of envisioning. The text on *Vision* already alluded to the principal figure which captures much of the trend in architectural practice, beyond Eisenman's experimental and conjectural activities. He asks us to suppose for a moment that architecture could be conceptualised as a Moebius strip, with an unbroken continuity between interior and exterior. What would this mean for vision? Gilles Deleuze has proposed just such a possible continuity with his idea of the fold.

Eisenman added that Deleuze's fold is more 'radical than origami', because it contains no narrative or linear sequence. Although it should be noted that Deleuze explicitly mentions that the model for the science of matter is origami. Folding unfolds in space alongside of its functioning and meaning in space – it has what might be called an excessive condition of affect. This is what can be called the way of being, the event. Deleuze, which is also *a propos* for Eisenman, creates through recognition of the concept construction that is a world of interleavings, not a world of monocular perspectival perception, but a machine of seeing that is without history, and also without genesis and forces. The sole preoccupation is with effecting and the affect.

This is a philosophy of passage and not of ground, there is a singular composing and re-composing that transverses the chaos, not attempting to explain it, but solving and re-situating the multiplicative: in the movement, becoming and difference. For Deleuze there is a primacy of the *sentiendum*, and the differentiation does not determine the process of actualisation; it equally can be said to be the generator of problems, generating disjunctions while actualising tendencies which were contained in the original unity and compossibility.

Even in matter at the lowest degree of difference there is dilation and contraction, and even at the smallest scale there is always movement. Thus for matter one can speak of generalised vibration, vibrating matter, energy, and difference is nothing more than a difference of degree.

It is most likely from his reading of the contention in Deleuze's text *Le Pli*, that Eisenman derives his proposal, namely that the criterion or the operative concept of the baroque is the fold. It is in the baroque that the fold has unlimited freedom. Deleuze argues that the baroque invents infinite work or process,

[2]

Coop Himmelb(l)au, Delivery Centre,
MW Welt, Munich, 2000-2007. Design
model.

OMA, Parc de la Villette, 1982. Fragment
model.

[1]

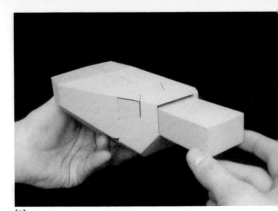

[2]

[3]

[4

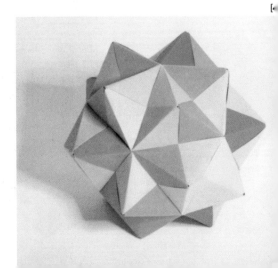

1 MVRDV, Berlin Voids, 1991. Model.
2 OMA, Casa da Musica, 2001. Concept
model.
3 G. Bruyns, origami experiment, 2008.
Photo: G. Bruyns, 2008.
4 Origami Modular Star.

that is expressive matter with different scales, speeds, vectors, it determines and materialises form, it produces inflection, the curve with a unique variable.

The smallest unit of matter is then the fold. The continuous does not separate into parts of parts, but rather is divided to infinity into smaller and smaller folds; a continuous labyrinth not dissolving into points, but rather a continuous consistent bending and responding to consistent and conspiring surroundings.

Where the organism is defined by endogenous folds for inorganic matter, the exogenous folds are always determined by the surrounding environment. The difference between organic and inorganic is a difference of vector. The inorganic goes towards greater and greater masses in which statistical mechanisms are operating the organic towards increasingly polarised masses in which the force of an individuating machinery, an internal individuation is applied. An organic body confers an interior on matter.

It is never then a question of essence and substance, in the sense of a real essence being a set of properties that determine all the other properties, dispositions, of a thing; rather it is a question of traits and operative functions, so that Deleuze can argue that in the fold there is a double differentiation, *per analogiam* two floors, and there is a movement along two infinite pleats of matter, so that there is matter amassed according to a first type of fold, and organised according to another.

The problem of the continuous labyrinth of matter and its parts, and of freedom of the soul in its predicates, which is what constitutes the two floors of Deleuze's figure, raises the conceptual problem of continuity, passage, the correspondence and communication between the two levels. Deleuze reads this against any form of nominal essence, where there is a complex going-together of substratum and idea which determines a sort of species; rather, in the baroque, matter tends to spill over into space, and there is a reconciliation with fluidity, and liquidity is divided into masses. In a sense Deleuze has taken a principle which allows him a deterritorialisation, so that he identifies the baroque in Dubuffet, Klee, etc. His single conceptual token: 'the fold'. Thus one has a great baroque montage, moving between floors, the lower pierced with windows, the upper blind and closed but vibrating.

Wölfflin has noted the material traits of the baroque: the horizontal widening of the floor; flattening of the pediment; the low curved stairs that push into space; matter handled as aggregates; the direct avoiding of perpendiculars; the elimination of the ornament of the jagged-edged acanthus; the use of limestone and spongy cavernous shapes, and vortices in which there is a renewed turbulence. Wölfflin had also noted the crucial problem of the expression of matter in his *Prolegomena to a Psychology of Architecture.*[62]

Studying the nature of fluids is itself the polar opposite of analysing well-defined shapes. It is the drama of contrast of water and stone. How could one formulate actual measured relation-

62 This can be found in: **Empathy, Form and Space: Problems in German Aesthetics, 1873-1893** (Malibu, Ca.: Getty Center, 1994), introduction and translation H.F. Mallgrave, and E. Ikonomou, as: 'Heinrich Wölfflin: Prolegomena to a Psychology of Architecture', pp.149-190.

ships for a continuum? In the paintings of Francis Bacon, Deleuze sees how the disruptions and assault on the narrative, even the figurative, allow the emergent to eventuate. This will materialise in figures that are no longer within the traditional play of representations, representations that anyway could never deliver what they claimed.

One can say that the body becomes disorganised, and the figure is a focus of vectors that move and lacerate, shape and play as the painterly sensation and ductus itself, the figure dissolving as it appears, dissipating into the field of colour. The lines of flight are the moments of escape, the actualising of the virtual, and there is an escape through each figuring, be it washbasin, umbrella, self-portrait.[63]

Here we see a reading which delineates the reaction; again this is directly applicable for Eisenman, to the illusions that bind the human from its 'overcoming', not the death of the subject, but the evacuation and escape from what has falsely bound it, largely ideas of the organism, significance, and the notion of the subject itself.

Deleuze and Guattari, in their commitment to the relation of creation and freedom, see these as the fundamental obstructions; organism, signification, subjectivation. Organism requires discipline and articulation of the body in such and such a way, any deviation is monstrous or renders you deviant; signification requires that you bear meaning and be inserted where you interpret and are interpreted, knowing oneself being no longer an awareness of the powers of affect and their belonging to powers but rather a kind of sturdy referendum in which you vote and are voted on; and thirdly the high imperative, 'be a subject', otherwise you are a miscreant, vandal, tramp, unrecognisable.

This is where Deleuze battles with the Hegelian power of recognition and the negative, culminating in self-awareness as absolute knowledge. We rob ourselves of vital existence through privileging the modes of the subject as personal and meaningful, and lose the cosmic contact with the impersonal plane of forces and energy which irradiates in image and actualisations that are becoming. For Deleuze and Guattari the artist allows the virtual manifest as life, and escapes from this. Of all the obstacles the most recalcitrant is the body, lived organism itself. In considering vital energy, it is 'inorganic, germinal and intensive'.

What is understood by vital energy is in effect the production and creation of difference, creation as the willed affirmation of difference. Things differ from themselves out of the 'explosive force' they carry within themselves, not because a thing differs from what it is not, or the objects to which it is said to relate.

---

63 Deleuze, **Francis Bacon: logique de la sensation**, vol.1 (Paris: Éditions de la Différence, 1981); **Francis Bacon: The Logic of Sensation**, trans. D.W. Smith (London: Continuum, 2003).

[1]

[2]

1 G. Bruyns, 'Moment of escape', water escaping from basin, 2008. Photo: G. Bruyns.

2 Francis Bacon, Self-portrait, 1973. Oil on canvas, 198 x 147.5 cm. Private collection.

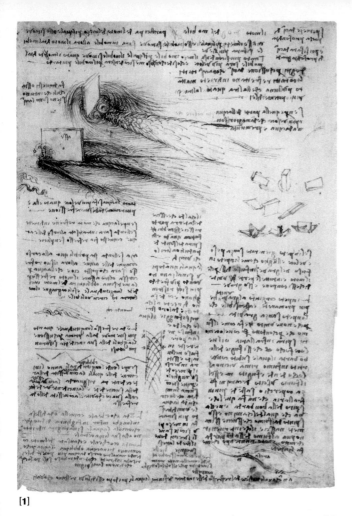

[1]

[2]

1 Leonardo da Vinci, Studies of flowing water, c. 1509-1511. Red chalk, pen and ink, 290 x 202 mm. No watermark. RL 12660.

2 Leonardo da Vinci, Studies of flowing water, c. 1509-1511. Red chalk, pen and ink, 205 x 203 mm. Watermark: eight-petalled flower (cut), not in Briquet. RL 12661.

The dynamic of acting and producing becomes obscured through the evolution of practical needs; we conflate our calculation and dive into a description of reality, which is continuous and indivisible. Rather than being thought of in the flow of life, organisms get characterised as things and discrete units. In the intrinsic power of expression the individual expresses more or less the immanent whole.

Deleuze argues that many of our false problems stem from the fact that we cannot go to the real. It is obstructed for us. Habit is the only failure because it sustains ignorance of the real in its blocking of the creature's ability to express the becoming of the creation which it is capable of expressing. Partly this arises from the fact that, even where in the intrinsic power of expression of the individual there is more or less the immanent whole, the whole cannot be represented. If the whole is not giveable, this is because it is the open, or because its nature is to change constantly, or to give rise to something new.

For Deleuze the givenness of the given is only a process, and it is constantly transformative. Actualisation belongs to the virtual, and virtual differentiation creates what it actualises; it is not simply the result of the possible. The actual is constituted, the virtual constitutes. This notion of creation, Hallward shows, has three aspects in Deleuze: 1) there is first a pure impulse, an *élan* of creativity itself, inexhaustible source of pure potential or transformation. It figures as an inconceivable point of pure compressed intensity. 2) This pure impulse is conceivable through infinite diverse explication, through distinct creations; it distributes as vehicles for its manifestation or expression, virtual configurations, modal essences, degrees of power, events and ideas. 3) Determination of material existence of constituted bodies, states of affairs, articulated propositions. Hallward adds, what accounts for an individual is not the presentable characteristics of what is thus individuated but the dynamic process of individuating itself, for instance the process whereby an embryo develops into an organism, a liquid solution into a crystal, or a bubble into a sphere.[64]

The virtual is intensive, constituting, spiritual. The virtual is more real than the actual. Virtual assemblages, unlike an extensive one that can be subdivided without changing the divided thing, are in constant flux, the qualities of which depend on the set as a whole: the best example is the weather: actual at any present moment, but only because of dynamic motion of atmospheric forces as a whole. This motion or force cannot be grasped simply by measuring a series of actual states of affairs to which it gives rise as motion or energy; it exists in intensive rather than extensive form. Virtual materiality eventuates in the work of Guattari and Deleuze in a series of novel configurations: rhizome, *haecceity*, abstract machine, nomadic distribution, body without organs, smooth-space.

The latter is very much of moment to Eisenman, and is characterised by Deleuze as a space filled by events, or *haecceities*, far more than by formed and perceived things. It is a space of

64 Peter Hallward, **Out of this World** (London: Verso, 2006). Also see T. Clark, 'A White-headian Chaosmos: Process Philosophy from a Deleuzean Perspective', in **Process Studies** 28, 3-4, 1999, pp.179-194.

affects, more than one of properties. Intense *Spatium* instead of *Extensio*. A body without organs instead of an organism.

The singularity of the event is germane to understanding the poetry of Gerald Manley Hopkins, who coined 'inscape' and 'instress' as equivalents of the Scotian *haeccitas*, an emphatic thisness of the this, which for Hegel has been consigned to an empty moment of empiricism's false knowledge.[65]

Creation cannot be reduced just to an object or cause, as the example of the event: a time, a life, a season, an atmosphere, degrees of heat, an intensity of white, a herd, a swarm, shows. The alignment to the creative allows the impersonality of the event to effectuate. Further, the account of the non-organic life that grips the world and the creation of 'pure vital energy' cohere on a plane that excludes the organism, thus the creative body is a virtual one, a body without organs. The body without organs does not have any actual organisation of its organs beneath the molar and strategically identified body and organisation. There are innumerable molecular and larval sub-identities; this is the real non-organic substance of the body. For Deleuze this also indicates that we are a badly analysed mixture. Every living being is a multiplicity and must live as such.

The example of the embryo is given: 'The destiny and achievement of the embryo is to live the unliveable, to sustain forced movements of a scope that would break any skeleton'. Guattari and Deleuze add that a pure spatio-temporal dynamism can only be experienced at the border of the livable, observing that there are systematic vital movements, *torsions*, only the embryo can sustain; an adult would be torn apart by them. There are movements for which one can only be a patient, and the patient in turn only a larva. Thought is one of those terrible movements which can be sustained only under the condition of a larval subject; the philosopher is a larval subject of his own system.

The post-human is the effective redemption from the human, the *Überwindung* of Nietzsche's *Übermensch*; that is, the one who goes across, transcends without the transcendental. Man's own self-overcoming is to return to the open, to become an event of affirmation and expression. The actual on this account literally flees from the static dualisms of rhizome-arboreal, nomad-sedentary, minor-major, noble-base. The actual contains then a counter actualising energy which individuates the virtual. The event brings back the possibility of the seeming and shining, the light of things. As in archaic phenomenological thinking, the appearance is Apollo.

It may still be possible to ask what this uncaused illumination effects, what is

---

65 See diary entry from May 14, 1870: 'Wych-elms not out till today. The chestnuts down by St. Joseph's were a beautiful sight; each spike had its own pitch, yet each followed in its place in the sweep with a deeper and deeper stoop. When the wind tossed them they plunged and crossed one another without losing their inscape. (Observe that motion multiplies inscape only when inscape is discovered, otherwise it disfigures)', from: W.H. Gardner, **Gerald Manley Hopkins** (London: Penguin Books, 1953, p.122).

[1]

[2]

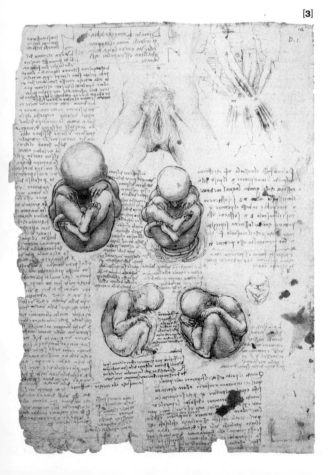

[3]

1 Francis Bacon, Three Figures and a
Portrait, 1975. Oil on canvas,
198.1 × 147.3 cm. Tate Collection, London.
2 Spherical bubble structures of cham-
pagne. Photo: G. Bruyns.
3 Leonardo da Vinci, The embryo in utero,
c. 1511-13. Black and red chalk under-
drawing, pen and ink, some wash,
305 × 220 mm. No watermark. RL 19101.
Next Pages Photos taken of models made
by students in the recently destroyed Faculty
of Architecture, Delft University of Technology. Photo: G. Bruyns, 2008.

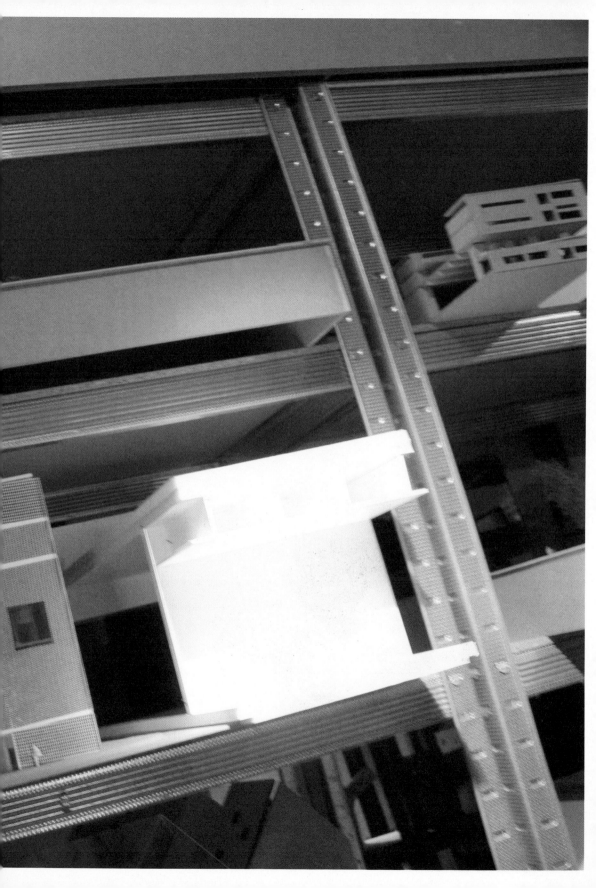

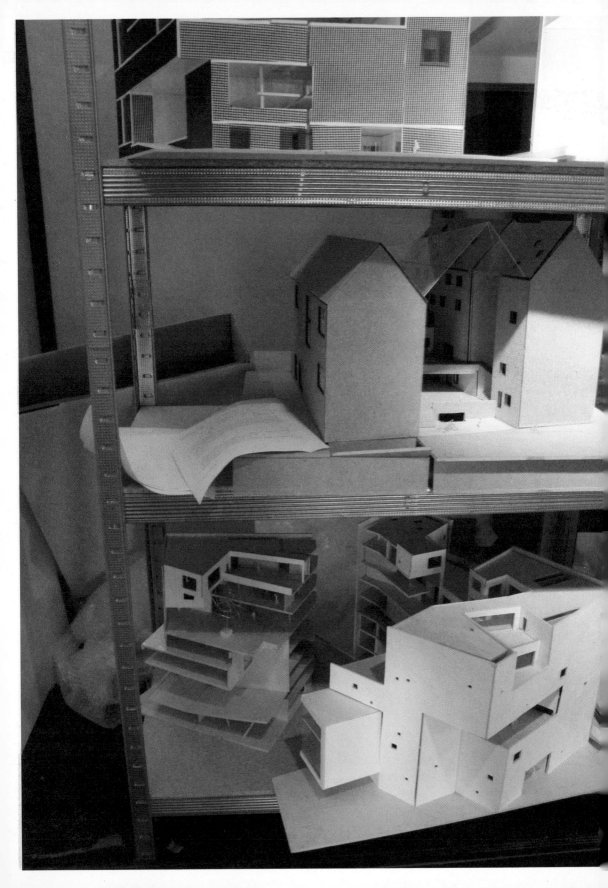

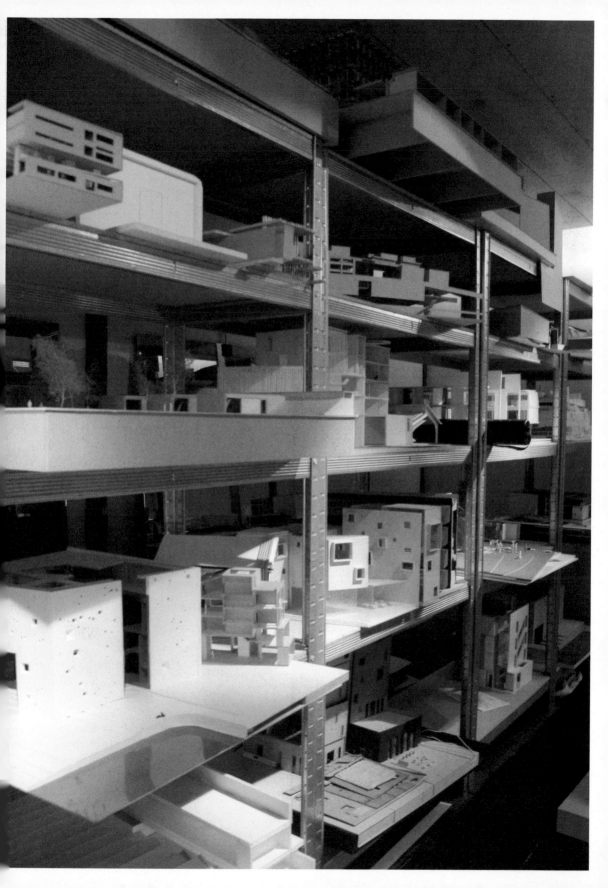

demanded for the open of this becoming? For Deleuze the radical request is to seek in the indeterminacy of the possibility of sensation, the demand that we look 'to sensation' for the conditions of the possibility of thought. Here the unknowing is not a question of lack of knowledge, but the refusal to be determined by the ontology of the great object, of the significant, or nihilist subject. It, the unknowing, is the event that is not denumerable, it is *inachève*, vague, and makes us into singular essences. Thus the multiplicity is a potential for bifurcation and variation in an open whole. Drawing from his interpretation of Spinoza, Deleuze reads the body as a nexus of variable connections, a multiplicity. The body is not a form, but a complex relation between differential speeds, between a slowing and acceleration of particles. This relation varies between bodies and within bodies, and bodies are immensely complex, made up of differential rhythms and affective intensities and so, in that sense too, a body is only made up of particles and affects and is without organs.

The virtual mobilises unspecified singularities, bringing them into an indeterminate plan. Virtual construction frees forms, figures, activities from an a priori determining or grounding, it departs from the kind of organ-isation that tries to set things out in advance; it constructs a space whose rules can themselves be altered through what happens in it. This performativity, improvisation, is the creation of a dynamic space that is prior to any qualification, it too belongs to the region of the open.

The question of the open in Heidegger and in Deleuze can be compared. For Deleuze, his understanding of a variation in an open whole, creation itself, gives us a complex lexis; *haeccitas*, firstness, freshness, vagueness, nomadism, *voisinage*, dispersal, sense, unfolding.

For Heidegger this is not a movement 'out' of world, but a 'being into' world, which is the free choice of *Dasein* that looks upon what is in freedom, a freedom that is carried out in an open space, understood as a lighted glade, i.e. in disclosedness. All disclosive looking comes out of an open space, goes into an open space, and brings us into an open space. The freedom to enter the open space neither consists in the unbounded arbitrariness of a free will, nor is it simply bound to occur by law. The openness of the open space conceals whilst lighting up.

In Heidegger's account it is the exercise of freedom that makes the open available for *Dasein*. That is to say that for something to be available to us to look upon, it must stand in a cleared and open space, for which Heidegger uses the term *Lichtung*. This has the meaning of a clearing, such as one might find in a forest, where there is an opening. In the self-offering of Being such a *Lichtung* occurs, and the exercise of human freedom is to participate in the availability of this clearing, to bring the disclosive look of *Dasein* to that which is offered in the clearing.

As the appearance of light is ignored in favour of what is seen, so the nearness of Being in its showing is literally by-passed with a concentration on beings. As *Dasein* we overlook the open, because the very disclosure of Being is a veiling towards what is shown, a veiling in favour of beings. The notion of re-vealing has a sense of the parting of veils, the revelation. Within the mystery of Being, it is also a concealing. We are literally aware of the veiling, and the disclosure of Being is available to us in this way of revealing and concealing, of which we gain a glimpse, or see it in a glance.[66]

What much of this discussion points to is the complex way in which architecture is considered in relation to space. Perhaps one of the clearest accounts of the problem so construed is found in Langer's *Feeling and Form*, where she discusses the modes of virtual space.[67] This text, published in 1953, already pointed to the significance of the virtual for architecture, some thirty years before the engagement of Eisenman, and later Gehry, with this phenomenon.

Langer's point of departure in the discussion is the immensely influential text of Hildebrand,[68] who took the notion of perceptual space and treated it as a scene, and that this perceptual space was created through purely visual forms, creating unexpected transpositions, where he argues for example that as the painter's problem of form is the creation of apparent volume by means of a two-dimensional surface, so for the sculptor it is the creation of a two-dimensional picture plane by means of actual volume.

What Langer identifies as mistaken in Hildebrand's theory is the way in which he passes from a special theory of pictorial space to the concept of perceptual space in general, taken to underlie all the 'plastic arts' and making them one family. For Langer the primary illusion is not the scene, which is only one of its articulations, rather it is virtual space.[69] Pictorial art should not be treated as the measure of all plastic expression, but one should look to sculpture for its own version of virtual space, and to architecture for its own.

It is obvious in painting that a flat surface creates a three-dimensional space that is obviously virtual. Even if Hildebrand's theory seems satisfied by the claim that the sculptor presented a three-dimensional object in the two-dimensional picture plane of perceptual space, Langer doubts if sculptors think in terms of pictures or ideal planes, ideal planes of vision staged one behind another to define deep space. She argues instead that sculpture is essentially volume even when it is wedded to a background.

However, the volume is not a cubic measure. It is a space made visible, and thus she argues is more than the area which the figure actually occupies. The tangible form has a complement of empty space which is in fact part of the sculptural volume, the void enfolds it, and the enfolding space has vital form as a continuation of the figure. It is the semblance of organism and vital function that the illusion of sculptural volume has as its primary principle.

Only the form of life has a necessity, it achieves certain forms inevitably as it goes along. Even carved wood is dead matter. Only its form is the form of life, and the space it makes visible

66 The most detailed recent discussion of this can be found in: Malpas, **Heidegger's Topology: Being, Place, World** (MIT Press, 2007).
67 Susanne K. Langer, **Feeling and Form: A Theory of Art** (New York: Charles Scribner's, 1952).
68 For Hildebrand's 'The Problem of Form in the Fine Arts', see note 62.
69 Langer, **op cit.**, p.87.

Hans Holbein the Younger, The Ambas-
sadors, 1533. Oil on wood, 207 × 209.5 cm.
National Gallery, London.

is vitalised as it would be by organic activity at its centre. It is virtual kinetic volume created by and with the semblance of living form.

What is at issue is the expression of biological feeling and not of biological function, and it is this expression which communicates the semblance of the inevitable, necessary, inviolable, organising the space it fills, and also the space that seems to touch it and be necessary to its appearance.

Tactile space is made visible. This is the source of the powerful abstraction from actual objects, a construction in three dimensions which is the semblance of kinetic space. This is organised in each person's experience as environment. The body is its centre and the point of orientation from which the world of tangible reality is plotted: objects, distances, motions, shape, size and mass. This results in a pithy formulation: sculpture is literally the image of kinetic volume in sensory space. However, we see the sculpture as a centre of space all its own, even as we think of it as an object.

Where painting creates an illusory scene, and sculpture an illusory organism, there is a third mode of creating virtual space, yet just as commandingly artistic, and in its scope the most ambitious of all; this is architecture.[70]

Langer argues that the 'illusion' of architecture is easily missed, because of the importance of its values: shelter, comfort, safekeeping. The sheerness of its practical functions has led architecture to be confused about its very status. For some it is chiefly utilitarian, or it is applied art where the ideal that one begins with is inevitably compromised in the reality of making, and some have argued that utility and function are paramount. Langer notes perspicuously that in architecture the problem of appearance and reality comes to a head as in no other art.

Architecture is a plastic art and its first achievement is always, even if unconsciously, an illusion, that is, something imaginary or conceptual translated into visual impressions. Her argument is that, where scene is the basic abstraction of pictorial art, and kinetic volume of sculpture, that 'of architecture is an ethnic domain'. By domain she does not mean a thing among things, but rather a sphere of influence of a function or functions. In this view a ship is a self-contained place, as is a Gypsy camp, an Indian camp, or a circus camp, however often it shifts its geodetic bearings. Literally the camp is in a place and culturally it is a place; and a place, in this non-geographical sense, is a created thing, 'an ethnic domain made visible, tangible, sensible'.[71]

What, one may ask, is the illusion of which Langer insists? It is primarily an illusion of self-contained, self-sufficient, perceptual space. The principle of organisation is its own, that is, it is organised as a functional realm made visible, the centre of a virtual world – 'the ethnic domain' – and itself a geographical semblance.

The organising power can be seen, for example, with the temple of Poseidon at Sounion: the outside world becomes its visible context, the horizon its frame. A tomb may create a complete

70 Ibid., p.92.
71 Ibid., p.95.

domain, and the created place is a semblance. The tomb carved out of a solid rock could contain the world of the dead, having no outside, with proportions internally derived, from the stone, from the burial, and 'define an architectural space that may be deep and high and wide, within a few cubits of actual measure'. Therefore the created place is a semblance, and whatever effects that semblance is architecturally relevant.

However, a universe created by man and for man 'in the image of nature' – Langer is drawing from Le Corbusier – is not created by simulating natural objects, but by exemplifying the laws of gravity, of statics and dynamics, and this is the spatial semblance of a world, because it is made in actual space; yet is not systematically continuous with the rest of nature in a complete democracy of places. It has its own centre and periphery, not dividing one place from all others, but limiting from within whatever there is to be. That is the image of an ethnic domain, the primary illusion in architecture.

If the house has been the builder's elementary school, great architectural ideas, Langer avers, have rarely arisen from domestic needs. Such architectural ideas as the temple, the tomb, the fortress, the hall or the theatre grew from the fact of the social collective, and its domain was essentially public. When made visible the image is a public realm in architecture.

Most early architecture – megalithic mounds, temples of the sun, which define what might be called religious space – constitutes a virtual realm. The temple symbolises the corners of the earth, or when it dominates a whole town or city its outward appearance organises the site of everything else, because it is the confluence of all ideas. Architecture creates the semblance of the world, which is the counterpart of a self. It is a total environment made visible where the self is collective, as in a tribe; its world is communal, for personal selfhood, it is the home. As the actual environment of a being is a system of functional relations, so a virtual environment, the created space of architecture is a symbol of functional existence. This does not mean however, that signs of important activities – hooks for implements, convenient benches, well-planned doors – play any part in its significance. In that false assumption lies the error of 'functionalism': it does not lie very deep, but perhaps as deep as the theory itself goes.

Langer suggests that what is gained for architecture in her proposition is the primary illusion of plastic art. Virtual space appears in architecture as envisagement of an ethnic domain that can be listed under three considerations. First, it frees architecture from the bondage of special factors of construction, even the

1 Le Corbusier inspecting a model of **à redent** housing.
2 Le Corbusier, illustration showing the principle of the Unité d'Habitation, c. 1950
3 Le Corbusier, model for project for Venic Hospital, 1963.

1]

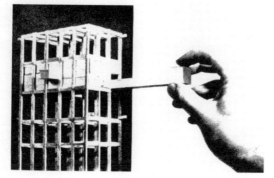

[2]

[3]

[1]

[2]

[3]

1 Le Corbusier, competition project for the
Soviet Palace in Moscow, 1931-32.
Photograph of original model.
2 Eric Mendelsohn, model for Palace of the
Soviets competition, 1931.
3 Eric Mendelsohn, model for Palace of the
Soviets competition, 1931.

elementary ones of pier, lintel and arch. Here she suggests that such technical features may yield to other ones and the creation that takes shape may be pure and unquestionable architecture. Secondly, she advances the claim that the building proceeds from the inside to the outside, and the façade is like the skin or carapace of a living creature, being the outer limit of a vital system, a protection against the world and a point of contact and interaction with the world. In the third place, it provides a criterion for what is essential to architecture, what belongs as essentials or variables. For example, furnishing belongs to architecture insofar as it takes part in creating the ethnic domain. Pictures treated by 'interior decorators' as embellishments in a room may remain, she notes, dislocated from it or even hostile; yet a great picture has a right to a room, and a space frankly consecrated to it is an ethnic domain of a special sort. Many practical arrangements can be built into a house, which affect the utility of the building but not its semblance, and so they are material factors and not architectural elements, although they are nevertheless the architect's concerns.

It is possible, thanks to the researches of Bruce Lindsey, to look in some detail at what he has called *Digital Gehry*, and the way in which the virtual context has become more available to architects in their design practice. In the case of Gehry one also has the *exemplum* of the fluent practice of what Lindsey calls the adaptation of digital tools.[72]

Once again, Gehry adverts to the process of his own making, and to the products of that process, drawings and models, which for him function as in painting, where there is a making up of one's mind. He places this decisionist and active gesture as the principal feature of design.

Partly there is a specific Aristotelian provenance in what Gehry has to say, since like Aristotle he recognises that the architect indeed may not do any building at all, rather others depend on his *eidos* to guide them in the work. Thus, Gehry suggests that it is indeed drawings and model-making that are the last vestiges of 'the master builder'. It is drawings and models which become the analogues of construction. Throughout, these media are referred to as tools, which are characterised by their different degrees of abstraction.

In considering drawing, Gehry thinks of the abstraction as controlling complexity. The degree of abstraction is controlled through modelling, be it two-, three- or even four-dimensional. It should be noted that this emphasis on the abstraction of drawing may very well stem from those drawings that belong to scientific and industrial processes. One can observe there is a movement away from representing the object to indicating movement itself, or process, as one has in graphs and flow-charts, and as Dubrey and Willats have suggested, with the invention of printed circuits the drawing and the object become consubstantial.

The logic circuit in a computer is at once a drawing of the logic and the electric circuit by which the logic is effected. It is maps that have tended to occupy the middle ground between

72 For Gehry, I have drawn on: Bruce Lindsey, **Digital Gehry** (Basle: Birkhäuser, 2001); B.J. Novitiski, 'Gehry Forges New Computer Links', in **Architecture**, August 1992. See especially: F. Dal Co and K.W. Forester, **Frank O. Gehry: The Complete Works** (New York: Monacelli Press, 1998); D.A. Schon, **The Reflective Practitioner: How Professionals Think in Action** (New York: Harper Collins, 1983). See also: A. Zaera, 'Frank Gehry 1991-95: Conversations with Frank O. Gehry', in **El Croquis**, no.74-5, 1995; D. Willis, **The Emerald City and Other Essays on the Architectural Imagination** (New York: Princeton Architectural Press, 1999).

pictorial representation and mathematical abstraction. However, they too have become progressively more mathematical, that is, schematic, and open up new possibilities in schematic drawing. Gehry draws a sharp contrast between this and the model. The main function of the model is that it simplifies and aids with communication. Here communication is said to operate as an extension of perception.

In the mode of abstraction the drawing searches for possible correspondences, and this is the skill of the artist, since the more abstract the drawing, the more likely it may provoke correspondences that could not have been predicted in advance. The model, on the other hand, emphasises the totality of a situation due to its small size, and it also encourages re-arrangement. In that sense it is more specific than drawings, because it exists in space, as we do.

A further claim is that there is an indeterminacy in drawings, in that they are seen as fragments of larger wholes. For Gehry there is a highly modulated inter-relation between drawing and talking to the client and the use of words, sounds and pictures. He points out that his drawing is not that of a structural engineer:

I do a different kind of drawing. They are searching in the paper. It's almost like I am grinding into the paper, trying to find the building.

He continues to expand this analogy to the work of a sculptor:

It's like a sculptor cutting into the stone or marble trying to find the image … it's a frantic kind of scratching. I let that lead, and then make models of the ideas scratched out on the paper, and then go back to the drawing and so on.[73]

However, the drawing is not an end in itself, unlike the beautiful drawings of Michael Graves, which are difficult to build: 'I always focus on a building, draw-ings are just stepping stones … and they do not even look like the building but I know what they are telling me to do.'

The procedure is similar to Eisenman: there is at first the stated abstraction, then a translation from the provoking correspondence through translation into a physical model. Then the model is regarded as being less abstract, made from actual materials, and thus even in this scale and minimum sense engaging one in 'material resistance'. Here another communicative effect is opened up, the ma-terial can provide material feedback.

   73 This is quoted in Lindsey, **Digital Gehry**, p.26.

[1]

2]

[3]

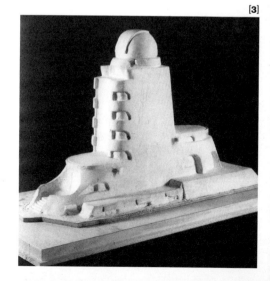

Le Corbusier, original model for
tre Dame du Haut chapel, Ronchamp,
50-55. Wood, 30 × 58 × 51 cm.
Le Corbusier, Notre Dame du Haut
apel, Ronchamp, 1950-55. Working
del, floor and façade plans mounted on
rdboard, 24 × 32 cm.
Eric Mendelsohn, model of the Tower for
stein, 1917-21.

In Gehry's work his engagement with Easy Edge Furniture from the late 1960s and early '70s, largely made from corrugated cardboard, was an embodiment of the energy of material research. Thus included in the design process was the conception of material resistance, talking to the client, the architectural model, and because the models were easier to understand, being three-dimensional and environing space, they allowed the client to participate in a dialogue with the architect. As will become clearer, it is this insistence on the assembly of process, things and persons that captures for Gehry the architectural communication.

Gehry is committed to the broader symbolic, imaginative, virtual nexus in which the design process engages the value of the model and its incompleteness, its different level of abstraction from drawing, that it could be operated on and that its very incompleteness required active perceptual spatial participation.

What he means by this is well illustrated from his use of strings on the site model for the Davis House and Studio Malibu (California, 1972), which allowed him to create perspectival lines above the terrain. The understanding of the power of the model to allow the visualising of new arrangements can be deduced from his practice for the Loyola University Law School (Los Angeles, 1978), where fragments and programs of buildings saw a city-like composition develop in the arrangement of spaces, which created a sense of emergent community. Sorkin and Dal Co read the model that effectuated such envisioning as a 3D bubble diagram of functionally specific and spatially suggestive relations.

There Gehry used colour-coded block models which were compressed into a single building model, where individual blocks prompt re-arrangement. Indeed the models and the objects were taken as operating like Renaissance Memory Theatres, that is to say that the objects were placed in a theatre of memory associated with the dialogue to be remembered. One might also allude to the older sense in French of the idea of a representation as part of a theatre programme, so that the use of the models is a performative staging and storing of memory which is the fullness of the different inventions within the open dialogue.

When Gehry collaborated with sculptors such as Claes Oldenburg, Coosje van Bruggen and the landscape architect Peter Walker, one can see that the real tension and collision for the shifting design preoccupations is how to account for the development of forms between abstraction and things. The need to generate dynamic shapes also involved that objects were becoming more complex.

1 Frank Gehry, Davis Studio and Residence 1968-72. External view and plan.
2 Frank Gehry, Easy Edge cardboard furniture, 1969-73.
3 Frank Gehry, Loyola Law School, Los Angeles, 1978. Site model.
4 Frank Gehry, Burns Building, Loyola Law School, Los Angeles, 1978. Sketch of façade.

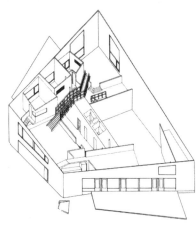

[1]

[2]

[3]

[4]

A fine example is the project for the Olympic Village in Barcelona 1992, which included a 54m long and 35m high fish-shaped canopy, part of a 14,000 square metre development designed by Gehry. There was a tight production schedule of 10 months and the problem of creating such a complex object in a short amount of time and within budget.

Lindsey says that the design developed from Gehry sketches, which were then translated into a wood and metal model. The structural problem then arose as to how to construct a support for the fish. Computer software was used to model the complex form, which produced a digital model that was visually accurate; however, it lacked the necessary surface information to construct the form.[74] The surface of the Alias Software, defined as a grid of polygons approximating the shape, did not allow for the precise statical rotation of points on the surface.

Perhaps one of the most radical responses to the work of Gehry and even Eisenman can be traced in the architectural writings of Jean Baudrillard, where the conception of the object is considered in order to raise the possibility, as he puts it, of an architecture that would be capable of challenging space, society, architecture itself and the architect's illusion of mastery.

> If for example I consider the truth of a building like the World Trade Center, I see that even in the 1960s architecture was already generating the profile of a society and period which was hyperreal, if not yet actually computerised, with the twin towers resembling nothing so much as two strips of punched tape. In their twinness we might say today they were already cloned, and were indeed something like the death of 'the original'.

Baudrillard had also taken the twin towers as emblematic, disclosing of the new logic of a system where, in having two towers, the system of capital had signified the end of all reference, of all competition. Like the multiple replicas of Warhol's imagery, there is the death of the original and representation; it is also the triumph of the strategies of models and commutations:

> There is a particular fascination in this reduplication. As high as they are, higher than all the others, the two towers signify nevertheless the end of verticality. They ignore the other buildings, they are not of the same race, they no longer challenge them, nor compare themselves to them, they look one into the other as into a mirror and culminate in the prestige of similitude.

74 See note 72.

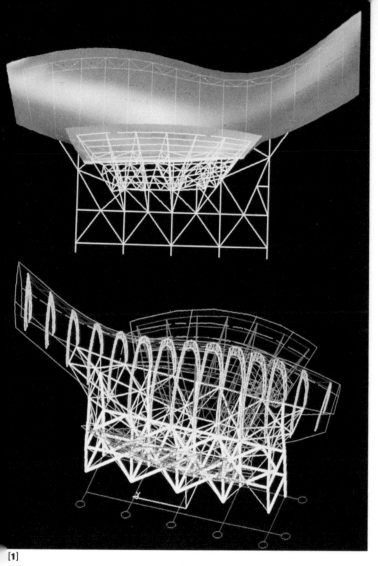

[1]

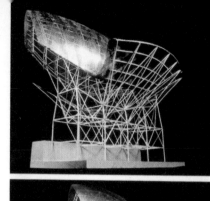

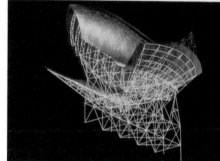

[2]

[3]

1 Frank Gehry, Olympic Village Monumental
Sculpture, Barcelona, 1992. CATIA model
and completed FISH Sculpture.
2 Frank Gehry, Olympic Village Monumental
Sculpture, Barcelona, 1992. CATIA Surface
model of FISH.
3 Frank Gehry, Olympic Village Monumental
Sculpture, Barcelona, 1992. Photograph of
FISH Sculpture.

What they project is the idea of the model that they are for one another, and their twin altitude presents no longer any value of transcendence. They signify only that the strategy of models and commutations wins out in the very heart of the system itself … there remains only a series closed on the number two, just as if architecture, in the image of the system, proceeded only from a unchangeable genetic code, a definitive model.[75]

With Gehry, Baudrillard confronts what he takes as the virtuality of architecture and the architecture of the virtual. Drawing on Wilhelm Flusser's hypothesis for photographic images, that the immense majority of them do not express the photographer's choice or vision but 'merely deploy the technical resources of the camera', Baudrillard sees in architectural practice a similar automatism emerging:

> …this is not simply a matter of materials and building techniques, it is also a question of models.[76]

Architecture does not need to refer to truth or originality, but merely to the technical availability of forms and materials, and Baudrillard adds:

> The truth that emerges is no longer even the truth of objective conditions. Still less is it the truth of the architect's subjective will. It is quite simply the truth of the technical apparatus and its operation. We may still choose to call this 'architecture', but it is not at all clear that it is genuinely so.[77]

To make his point he takes as his example the Guggenheim Museum in Bilbao: 'a virtual object if ever there was one, the prototype of virtual architecture'. Harbison reads it as exemplifying the baroque valorisation of the sketch.[78]

It is possible to turn again to earlier reflections in architectural discourse to assess what the shifts in the understanding of the model have been, as indicated in the above discussion, and to elaborate other readings within the tradition of architecture prompted by the new, which opens up such pasts for different inspection; perhaps we will see that the tension of the human body, the machine, and the intelligible paradigm occur throughout this history.

Given the paucity of allusions to the model, or reference to the use of models in Vitruvius' *Ten Books On Architecture*, his remarks in book x are valuable and instructive. The comments and asides on models and problems associated with their application can be found in the course of the narration of a dystopic and moralising anecdote about Diognetus, a Rhodian architect, that recounts his expertise and ingenuity during a siege of Rhodes, in which however the real war turns out to be, which is the point of the Vitruvian tale, between human resourcefulness and machines, with Vitruvius casting a backward glance at a time when it was decided in favour of the architects.[79]

It was precisely in such work, minding the machines of war that Vitruvius had first come to the notice of the father of the dedicatee of the *Ten Books*, Julius Caesar, and according to his preface it was the same work on which he was spending his time when writing the *Ten Books*, namely outfitting catapults, as well as the repair of all 'other sorts of war machines', for which he received a stipend from the Imperator which continued at the recommendation of 'your sister'.

It is in discussion of such machines that he spends his last 'perfecting' chapter, as he calls it, of the scrolls, bringing the work to a conclusion with a vivid affirmation for an architecture that is literally cleverer than the technical, which would expand its scope to include, as outlined in the first book, a wide education and a firm theoretical commitment.

The life of Diognetus, who is the beneficiary of an annual income from the Rhodians due to their admiration for his skill, is very much put upon by the visit of an architect called Callias from Arados, who lands in Rhodes, and 'upon arrival gave a presentation in which he pulled out a model of a fortification wall'. On top of this wall he set up a machine on a universal joint, which snatched a siege tower advancing towards the wall, and brought it inside the fortifications.

So impressed were the Rhodians with the new arrival and his clever display that Diognetus lost his honorarium and they transferred the distinction to Callias instead. The *chutzpah* of Callias had secured him admirable employment.

At about the same time King Demetrius, known as the Besieger of Cities, *Poliorcetes*, was preparing to wage war on the Rhodians, and took into his service a famous Athenian architect, Epimachus, who made a siege tower at great expense, involving enormous exertion and labour. Vitruvius recounts it was 120 feet high and 60 wide, reinforced with goatskin and rawhide, and able to withstand the impact of a 360 pound shot launched from a ballista. The siege tower was also enormously heavy; Vitruvius gives the weight at 360,000 pounds. The tale of the three architects Diognetus, Callias and Epimachus now becomes interwoven, and Vitruvius gives what sounds like reported speech on the response of Callias to the sudden threat posed by the lumbering siege tower of Epimachus.

Callias, clearly confronted by the monstrous engine, tells the Rhodians that he cannot carry it within the walls as he promised to do. The text of Vitruvius tellingly explains the reason for the Rhodians' deception:

75 **Jean Baudrillard**, ed. Francesco Proto (Wiley Academy, 2006), pp.86-7. Also see: J. Baudrillard, **Simulacra and Simulation**, trans. S.F. Glaser (Ann Arbor: University of Michigan Press, 1994), first published in 1981. Speaking of the Beaubourg, Baudrillard suggests that the new model is that of security, which will encompass the whole social field and is fundamentally a model of deterrence, p.61.
76 See my article 'Invention and the Technological Imperative', **Oase**, December 2007, and 'Technogenesis and the Inventive City', in G. Bruyns and P. Healy (eds), **De-/signing the Urban** (Rotterdam: 010, 2006).
77 See note 75.
78 Robert Harbison, **Reflections on Baroque** (London: Reaktion Books, 2002).
79 **Vitruvius: Ten Books on Architecture**, ed. I.D. Rowland, T. Howe (Cambridge University Press, 1999); B. Baldwin 'The Date, Identity and Career of Vitruvius', in **Latomus**, 49, 1990, pp. 425-34; A.F. Healy, **Pliny the Elder on Science and Technology** (Oxford: Clarendon, 1999).

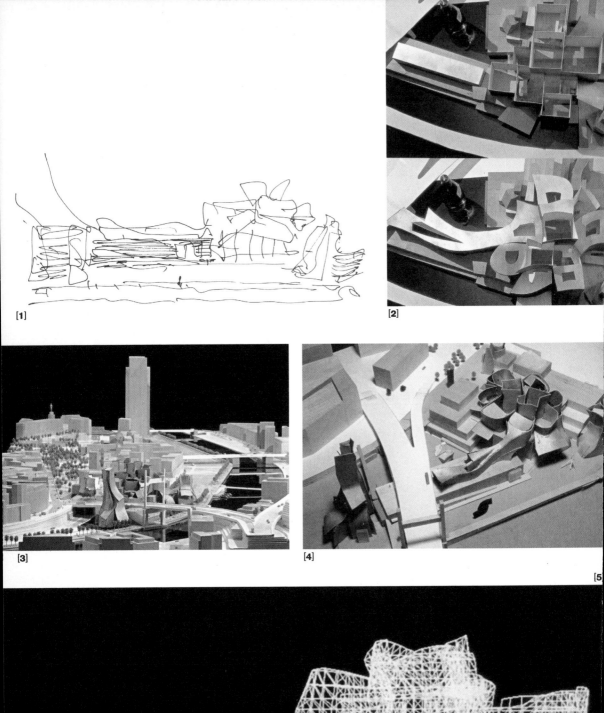
[1]

[2]

[3]

[4]

[5]

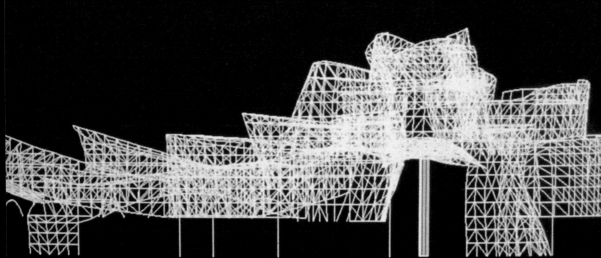

[6]

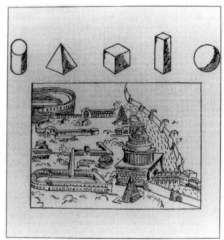

[7]

[8]

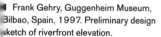

1 Frank Gehry, Guggenheim Museum,
Bilbao, Spain, 1997. Preliminary design
sketch of riverfront elevation.
2 Frank Gehry, Guggenheim Museum,
Bilbao, Spain, 1997. Design process
models.
3 Frank Gehry, Guggenheim Museum,
Bilbao, Spain, 1997. Urban context study
model.
4 Frank Gehry, Guggenheim Museum,
Bilbao, Spain, 1997. Original competition
model.
5 Frank Gehry, Guggenheim Museum,
Bilbao, Spain, 1997. CATIA structural steel
model.
6 Frank Gehry, Ray and Maria Stata Center,
Massachusetts Institute of Technology,
Cambridge, Mass., 1998. Massing model
and future development of surrounding area.
7 Sketch from **Vers une architecture** of
primary solids and Ancient Rome.
8 Le Corbusier, photo of original model for
Plan Obus, 1932.

...for not everything can be carried out according to the same principle. There are some things which achieve large-scale results like those achieved with small models. Then there are other things for which models cannot be made at all, and they must be built to scale in the first place.[80]

If it had been the extempore defence of Callias, it would have sounded like increasingly desperate rationalisation, but Vitruvius spells out the issue as clearly and completely as he can:

> There are some things that achieve large-scale results like those achieved with small models. And then there are other things for which models cannot be made at all, and they must be built to scale in the first place. And some things that seem perfectly realistic in a model vanish when their scale begins to be enlarged ... in some models things that seem to happen on a tiny scale might seem to occur on a larger scale as well, and that is how the Rhodians, deceived along the same lines, inflicted injury and insult upon Diognetus.[81]

The Rhodians beg back Diognetus who, after considerable entreaty, agrees on the condition he can keep the machine if captured, and proceeds then to defeat by a clever ruse the 'Besieger of Cities'.

His strategy was to make a breech in the wall towards which the siege engine was approaching and have as many Rhodians as possible dump water, mud and sewage through the pierced hole. Thus the next morning the engine churned up a sinkhole in the slime and came to a complete halt. Diognetus claimed his booty and later had it set up in public as a gift to the citizens, and as war *spolia*.

To discover how Vitruvius understands the model and its architecture, it is necessary to turn from this moralising tale to the earlier part of his work. Throughout, Vitruvius offers comments on his own work, occasionally entering personal considerations which are artfully aimed at the dedicatee to coax from him a favourable opinion, his self-effacement expressing skilled sycophancy and an ingratiating masochism. Thus he suggests that, unlike the enormously handsome Macedonian architect who made himself known to Alexander the Great and proposed to carve Mount Athos into the shape of a man, with the model of the city in one hand, Vitruvius is old, his face aged, but he can rely on his erudition to rescue the attention of another Imperator for his accounts.

Previous writing on architecture, as we learn from the preface to book IV, had left behind them precepts and volumes of commentaries on architecture that were not set in proper order but taken up instead as if they were stray particles. In the preface to book V however, Vitruvius draws attention to his task as one of writing for a readership which needs the obscurity of architectural terms and language to be condensed and exposed in a 'few crystal clear sentences', because the density of prose in architectural writing often serves to confuse the reader's mind. He has decided to write concisely so that people reading 'in their restricted leisure time may understand these points more quickly'. The unmistakable impression from this preface is that the writing is constructed to facilitate memorisation.

To this end he has also decided to follow a Pythagorean injunction, in which the Pythagoreans set down their precepts using the principle of cubes; they thought that two hundred and sixteen lines constituted a cube and there ought not to be more than three cubes in a single written composition. This piece of Pythagorean lore is not found in other testimonia, and along with the ascription of the famous theorem to Pythagoras is indeed only to be found in Vitruvius.

The interpretation offered by Vitruvius is intriguing: the cube is a body squared all round, made up of six sides whose plane surfaces are as long as they are wide. When thrown, the part on which it lands (so long as it remains untouched) preserves an immovable stability, 'the dice which the players throw onto the gaming board are like this'. We can possibly infer that Vitruvius here offers an illustration. This would be one of the 10 illustrations, none of which have survived, which were included in the original scrolls by Vitruvius.[82]

So he argues that Pythagoreans seem to have taken the image of the literary cube from dice, because this particular number of lines landing like dice on any side whatever will produce immovable stability of memory. That the locus for stability of memory should be taken from a game of chance is not the only unusual feature of this explanation. There is hardly any way of demonstrating that the principle is used, even in terms of the way in which the whole of the ten books is laid out.

The Pythagorean reference is not just a glancing allusion, but offers an important key to the whole work, whose structure is modelled in such a way that the text performs the theory of the writer and his principal intellectual allegiances. This following of the Pythagorean cubic principles 'will produce motionless stability of the memory there (*ibi*)'. The emphasis on *ibi* underlines that the cube dice rest and settle in a particular place or locus. It also requires that one take into view that these remarks are placed halfway through the scrolls, and this indicates, as in previous sections, a re-capitulation for the reader who is physically moving from scroll to scroll. It is then at the halfway point that Vitruvius adds this significant indication of his own working method and the model which guides his enterprise.

He clearly contrasts his own method with that of those authors who have written previously and who have, in his view, been very scattered and without system. Vitruvius adds yet another observation about the Pythagorean cubic principles, asserting that the Greek comic poets

80 Vitruvius, op. cit., Book X, ch.16.4.
81 Idem.
82 Guillaume de Philandrier in 1544 drew up a list of in-text illustrations suggested by Vitruvius, which for the most part did not survive in the manuscript tradition, suggesting nine or ten figures. In nearly all cases they are illustrations of elementary geometric diagrams. The fullest discussion of this and the Renaissance response of 'imaging' Vitruvius can be found in: Mario Carpo, see note 57. Carpo has also argued for the standardisation of urban form as a consequence of printed image in his 'Il cielo e i venti. Principi ecologici e forma urbana nel **De Architectura** di Vitruvio e nel vitruvianismo moderno', in **Intersezioni**, Rivista di Storie delle Idee XIII, April 1993, pp.3-41; C.H. Krinsky, 'Seventy-Eight Vitruvian Manuscripts', in **Journal of the Warburg and Courtauld Institutes**, XXX, 1967, p.43.

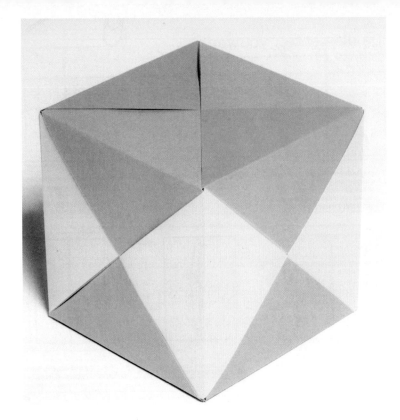

Origami Modular Cube.

divided up the 'space of their plays' by inserting a song by the chorus; defining the parts of the plays by the principle of the cube, they relieve the actor's speeches with these intervals. From this literary cube Vitruvius makes the decision to write in short volumes, to facilitate reading and memorisation of the text. He thus provides the most pithy summary to his various books in the prefaces. Being anxious to argue 'the excellence of our profession', Vitruvius has laid out in his first book what particular qualities it has, 'and in what disciplines the architect should be trained':

> I also added the reasons why one should acquire such skill ... Then I classified the main branches of architecture and I defined their contents. Then as a necessary first step, I explained, on theoretical principles, about walls and how healthful sites are chosen. I named the winds and showed, with illustrations, the regions from which each of them blows, I gave instructions about how to place avenues and side streets within the walls and then concluded the first volume. In the second I continued in the same vein, speaking of building materials, what uses they have in projects, and their respective properties according to Nature.

Having thus briefly outlined his writing in the first two books, Vitruvius turns his attention to speak about 'sacred dwellings' of the immortal gods and shall explain 'how they should be designed'.

At the beginning of the preface to the fourth *volumina*, Vitruvius returns again to summarise what he has laid out:

> In the third volume then I offered instruction about the design of temples, and about the variety of their types, which species they have and how many, and what the distribution of the various proportions ought to be according to type. Of those three types whose proportions exhibit the most intricate modular system I taught the conventions of the Ionic.

Indra Kagis McEwen has, in her *Vitruvius Writing the Body of Architecture*, drawn attention to the importance of writing for Vitruvius and his construction of the 'body' of architecture.[83] Following the suggestion of Pierre Gros, she has effectively provided a detailed exegesis for the claim made by Vitruvius in the Preface to Book IV:

> When I noticed, Imperator, that many who have provided rules and scrolls of commentaries on architecture have not left orderly works but only incomplete drafts, scattered like fragments, I decided it would be a worthy and most useful thing to bring the whole body of this great discipline to complete order and, in separate scrolls, develop a register of conditions for each of its different subjects....

83 Indra Kagis McEwen, **Vitruvius: Writing the Body of Architecture** (MIT Press, 2004).

Antoinette Novara, echoing Gros' emphasis, sees the work of Vitruvius as an act of service to Augustus, through the beneficial ordering of all architectural knowledge into a single well-ordered corpus. Indra Kagis McEwen wants to examine why such a corpus should be of such benefit. She points to the novelty of his use of the term 'corpus' and also to the 'opacity of the metaphor'; it is rarely used either by Cicero or Varro, the older contemporaries of Vitruvius.

In Book VI, Vitruvius repeated the metaphor and adds that he:

> [D]ecided to write the whole body of architecture and its principles with the greatest care, thinking it would not be an unwelcome service to all people.

The use of 'corpus' is key. Vitruvius uses it more insistently and differently than any other writers of the *Principiate*. The significance of the corpus of architecture becomes more weighted given the importance attached to one of the most commented-on metaphors of the whole work, namely the comparison of the temple with a body.

The thrust of McEwen's argument is that the birth of *architectura* as a clearly defined discipline appears to be codependent with the Roman project of world dominion. She also suggests, in what she terms an unsettling conclusion, that the body of architecture is the body of empire, and further that the principal aim of Vitruvius was to vindicate architecture's part in that project.

To demonstrate this precise political thesis, she reconfigures the work around different bodies: the angelic, the Herculean, the beautiful and the body of the king. The first division deals with the book as book, the second in Vitruvius' relation to August and Rome's Herculean task of civilising and conferring benefits which cannot be realised without his corpus. The third examines how beauty is decisive for 'forging the new world order', and finally by examining the statue of the Prima Porta, sculpted not long after Vitruvius' treatise, she argues that in *De architectura* the world body, the Prima Porta Augustus presents itself as an image. The sum of these bodies constitutes the ideological commitment of Vitruvius and makes of him *tout court* an ideologue of Empire.[84]

The notion of the first body relates to the structure of the text itself. It is in the xth book that he refers to the finished work:

> In this scroll I have given a complete account of the principles of the machines I consider most useful in times of peace and war. Now in the previous nine I brought together the ones for the other different subjects and parts, so that the whole body of architecture might have all its members developed in ten scrolls.

What is clearly of an unusual and reflexive kind here is that Vitruvius has already made the body the model for sacred building, and now places through the ten volumes a logic of construction which derives from principles that belong to a Pythagorean and Stoical philosophy.

The question that arises is, which body is significant for the corpus of writing? After all the body is composed by nature. It is not without significance that the notion of tempering and temple and template belong together, and that the role of *analogia* is crucial for the symmetry which is the basis for the composition of the temple. Dimensions of parts would relate to the whole, in the way a body does. Thus the face from the chin to the top of the hair line is one tenth of the total height of the body. Placing an outstretched palm from the wrist to the tip of the middle finger should be the same dimension. Thus the length of the face and hand are both a tenth of the complete unit, the body, which is equivalent to 1. The body itself is the primal unity. In Vitruvius' view, the ancients handed down a system of proportion in which the separate individual elements answer to the total form. The body again provides the template: when the well-formed body is stretched out or lying back with outstretched arms and feet within a circle, whose centre is at the navel, then the fingers and toes will trace the circumference of the circle as they move about.

However, Vitruvius adds that to whatever extent a circular scheme may be present in the body, a square design may also be observed there. It is this visualisation of a geometrical squaring of the circle which gives the human body its paradigmatic significance. It is the body in its smallest details, with commensurate proportions studied by painters and sculptors, which generated the principles of measure that grouped units of measure into the 'perfect number which the Greeks call *teleion*'. The ancients 'decided that the number called ten was perfect, because it was discovered from the number of digits on both hands'.

Vitruvius' theory of the origin of perfect numbers is speculative, and he hedges on the question of to what extent the outlaid body describes a circle, and he concludes that if it is agreed that from the limbs of the human body number was discovered, and that a correspondence of dimension exists among individual elements and the appearance of the body in its individual parts, then it is left for us to recognise that the ancients, who also established the houses of the immortal gods, ordered the elements of the works so that in both their shape and symmetry fitting dimensions of separate elements and of the work as a whole might be created. It is precisely on this analogy that Edmund Burke pours scorn in his *An Enquiry into our Ideas of the Sublime and Beautiful*.[85]

There is an evident circularity in the Vitruvian argument, since the well-formed body must already by definition have such connotation, that is, of a symmetry which is relevant for the composition. The claim which rests on the Vitruvian view of number, itself being generated from the hands, requires some comment.

The hands, then, provide the model for understanding from the body, and this privileged

84 Ibid., p.12.
85 E. Burke, **An Inquiry into our Ideas of the Sublime and Beautiful** (London: Dodsley, 1759), pp.181-86.

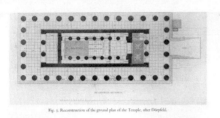

38. D'après Antonio Labacco, dessin de San Sebastiano portant la mention : «à Mantoue la main de Messere Battista Alberti».

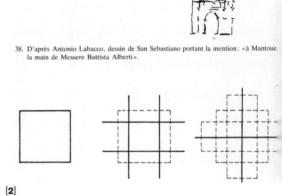

[1]

[2]

[3]

[4]

1 Reconstructions of plan, east elevation, a section and model of the Temple of Zeus.
2 Schema of the composition for San Sebastian.
3 Leonardo da Vinci, Vitruvian Man, c. 1485.
4 Five column orders according to Sebastian Serlio, 1537.

metonymy then literally points to the coherence of the design of the world. But the guiding principle is derived from the conception of the relation of parts and their relation to the whole. Indeed in referring to the study of the Greek painters and sculptors, Vitruvius is clearly aware that the famous *Kanon* of Polykleitos was both a statue and a treatise. Further Vitruvius extends his view of the importance of the body in architecture by applying the specific *analogia* again to the interpretation of the Doric column, which he sees as modelled on the proportions, strength and beauty of the male body, and the Ionic column on that of the female. In turning to the practice of Greek sculpture we may better understand what is at issue in Vitruvius' arguments. Following on that, it may be possible, as Robert Hahn has suggested, to work back from Polykleitos to earlier practices, and indeed to influence in the reverse direction, of architects on sculpture.

Philip Comar, in his *Images of the Body*,[86] thinks that the long-term consequence of this way of understanding the body leads to several consequences: that the basic system of architecture relies on a system of proportion and symmetry directly borrowed from the body and related to human form, and that this dependence reflects a desire to harmonise the material world offered to our senses and the pure forms distilled in the mind. The simplification, then, of living forms as metamorphoses into geometric solids implies that 'every form potentially contains the idea of a perfect model'. The famous Doryphoros is a treatise in marble or 'theorem in stone', as Comar phrases it.

Comar argues the dichotomous request for unity that the Ideal/real of Greek thinking required for the body. The ideal had its point of departure in the real human body, which for the male has been suggested as that of the warrior, and the Greek artist considered the figure as a whole; not, as with the Egyptian, according to a stance, but rather by capturing an animated pose. By taking in the poses Greek sculpture understood the body as occupying space. This was regulated by taking into account not just the front and side projections, but also contortions and angles, and allowing for illusionistic foreshortenings.

Nevertheless this still was the realisation of something approximate and which, despite the strongest naturalistic illusionism, was modulated through the fascination with geometry and number, as a way of indicating beauty through measure and measure as beautiful. As will be argued later, this cause of beauty and the relation to the mathematical is a significant feature of Aristotle's reading of the search for principles in his predecessors and especially among the 'so-called Pythagoreans'.

In Xenophon's *Memorabilia* there is a reference to Kleiton, a presumed Attic follower of Polykleitos (3, 10, 6-8), being questioned by Socrates, who according to tradition had been trained as a stone mason:

Isn't that right – what you are really imitating in human bodies is the frame drawn up or

86 Philippe Comar, **Images du corps** (Paris: Gallimard, 1993); translation Dorie and David Baker, **Images of the Body** (New York: Harry N. Abrams, 1999).

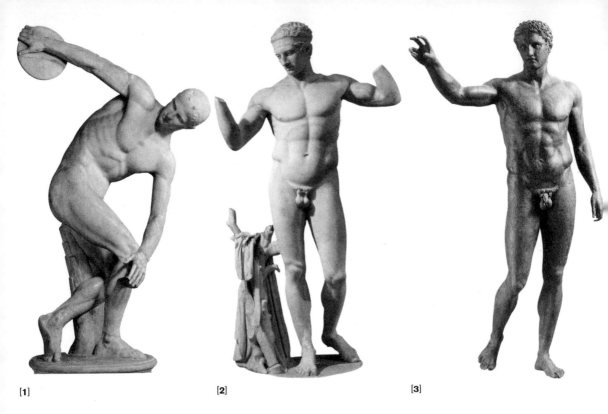

[1]   [2]   [3]

[4]

1 Diskobolus, copy after a Greek original ⌐
Myron c. 450 BC. Marble, 148cm high.
Museo Nazionale Romano, Rome.
2 Diadoumenos, the Youth Athlete, copy
after the bronze original by Polykleitos, 42⌐
BC. Marble, 186cm high. National Archae┐
logical Museum, Athens.
3 Youth of Anticytherus, mid 4th century
BC. Bronze, 194 cm high. National Archa┐
ological Museum, Athens.
4 Zeus or Poseidon, Cape Artemision, 46
BC. 209cm high. National Archaeological
Museum, Athens.

down, compressed and expanded by their posture, by the tensed and relaxed parts, and that is how you edge closer and convincingly towards their reality.

Here we have a double movement, which is also ascribed to the achievement of Polykleitos, that is to say there is a contracting and releasing simultaneously of the body, it is both tensed and relaxed, and these two oppositions are shown independently and consistently together. By abandoning the fixed grids with square fields as the instrument for measuring proportions, Comar maintains it was replaced by a supple system composed of flexible diamond shapes, which was taken as more capable of rendering active, asymmetrical, natural postures. The standing statue ceased to be rigidly frontal and formally balanced; instead it posed in contraposto, twisted in an S shape on the vertical axis, with weight on one leg, hips protruding, and muscles flexed. Grouped figures displayed tension and interplay of forms. An art of transition, the Greek ideal is based on a science of diagonals.

There is no consensus on how Polykleitos worked. Robert Hahn suggests that this is because of the fact that the canon not only supplied the 'nuts and bolts of the sculptor's art', but with the aesthetic dimension added something which depended on circumstance and actual working practice.

Rules have to be applied as one goes along. Haselberger has shown that for the architecture of the younger Didymaion, the paradigms incised on the temple walls themselves were refined as suited the workmen and modified as seen fit. Nevertheless, the paradigm illustrated the highest embodiment of the specified rule, and the aesthetic excellence consisted of instantiating those dimensions as far as possible. Thus Hahn interprets the concept of perfection:

…perfection says Polykleitos, according to Philon, is engendered by the near application of many numbers … *para micron-pollon arithmon.*

(The citation is from Philon Mechanicos, *Syntaxis*, 4.1.)[87]

In other words, there is a grid imposed over the block but the craftsman works according to feel as well. It seems fairly sensible that this working in smaller and smaller fractions added to the variety of sculptural production even when guided by a strict canon. It was used to demonstrate the theoretical application of a system of ideal proportions. *Kanon* also refers in Greek to a wooden measuring rod, a tool used by architects.

From the writings of Lucian, Pliny and Galen there is information about the treatise of Polykleitos, which has not survived. Galen's summary derives from his reading of Chryssipus, and the notion of the harmony of the body as health. However, it is not to Chryssipus that one

---

87 See the research of Robert Hahn, in D.L. Couprie, Robert Hahn, Gerard Naddas, **Anaximander in Context** (New York: SUNY Press, 2003).

needs to turn attention, but rather to the much more murky area of Pythagorean number religion.

Aristotle is still the chief ancient authority for the theory of the Pythagorean doctrine of the number 10 being perfect, because it was a result of the sum of the numbers 1, 2, 3 and 4, which form the *tetrakyts*, and an actual figure by which the Pythagorean brotherhood and sisterhood took the oath, as well as a principle of health. We find that Aristotle acknowledges in his discussion of book XIII of the *Metaphysics* the role of the mathematical in consideration of beauty:

> Now since the good and the beautiful are different (for the former always implies conduct as its subject, whilst the beautiful is found also in motionless things), those who assert that the mathematical sciences say nothing of the good or beautiful are in error. For these sciences say and prove a great deal about them; if they do not expressly mention them, but prove attributes which are their results or their definitions, it is not true to say they tell us nothing about them. The chief forms of beauty are order and symmetry and definiteness, which the mathematical sciences demonstrate in a special degree. And since these (e.g. order and definiteness) are obviously causes of many things, evidently these sciences must treat this sort of causative principle also (i.e. the beautiful) as in some cases a cause. But we shall speak more plainly elsewhere about these matters.

The most detailed surviving reference of Aristotle on the Pythagoreans is found at *Metaphysics* in book 1, where speaking of Plato's teachings, he adds:

> But he agreed with the Pythagoreans in saying that the One is substance and not a predicate of something else; and in saying that the numbers are the causes of the reality of other things he agreed with them; but positing a dyad and constructing the infinite out of great and small, instead of treating the infinite as one, is peculiar to him; and so is his view that numbers exist apart from sensible things; while they say that the things themselves are numbers, and do not place the objects of mathematics between Forms and sensible things....

And further, at 989b 30, Aristotle adds:

> The 'Pythagoreans' treat of principles and elements stranger than those of the physical philosophers (the reason is that they got the principles from non-sensible things, for the objects of mathematics, except those of astronomy, are of the class of things without movement); yet their discussions and investigations are all about nature; for they generate the heavens, and with regard to their parts and attributes and functions they observe the phenomena....

In the two direct references to Pythagoras in his extant writing, Aristotle seems to treat Pythagoras as a creature of legend; one reference in *Rhetoric* (1398b, 14), 'the Italian Greeks honoured Pythagoras', and the more extensive and informative passage in the *Metaphysics*, book I. Having discussed what is effectively a rapid review of previous philosophers including Hesiod, Empedocles, Leucippus Democritus, and their search for the principles of things, Aristotle adds that in thinking thus, 'there is a principle of things which is at the same time the cause of beauty, and that sort of cause from which things acquire movement':

Contemporaneously with these philosophers and before them, the so-called Pythagoreans, who were the first to take up mathematics, not only advanced this study, but also having being brought up in it they thought its principles were the principles of all things. Since of these principles numbers are by nature the first, and in numbers they seemed to see many resemblances to the things that exist and come into being – more than in fire and earth and water (such and such a modification of numbers being justice, another being soul and reason, another being opportunity – and similarly almost all other things being numerically expressible); since, again, they saw that the modifications and ratios of the musical scales were expressible in numbers; since then all other things seemed in their whole nature to be modelled in numbers, and numbers seemed to be the first thing in the whole of nature, they supposed the elements of numbers to be the elements of all things, and the whole heaven to be a musical scale and a number. And all the properties of numbers and scales which they could show to agree with the attributes and parts and the whole arrangement of the heavens, they collected and fitted into their scheme; and if there was a gap anywhere, they readily made additions so as to make their whole theory coherent, e.g. as the number ten is thought to be perfect and to comprise the whole nature of numbers, they say that the bodies which move through the heavens are ten, but as the visible bodies are only nine, to meet this they invent a tenth – the 'counter-earth'. We have discussed these matters more exactly elsewhere.

Aristotle did not deliver, it seems, on this last promise. However, many parts of his comments help to grasp what remains intrinsically paradoxical for understanding the body as a model, especially in light of the sculptural canon and the relation of number to movement. The argument leads to understanding how the conception of number and the organic are joined in practice, in the individual sculpture and in the temple itself viewed as an organic growth that is patterned.[88]

Spengler holds that the beginning and end of classical mathematics is consideration of the properties of individual bodies and their boundary surfaces; thus indirectly taking in conic sections and higher curves. The straight line for the Greeks is not an infinite continuum of points,

88 For a fuller discussion of these passages see: J.E. Raven, **Pythagoreans and Eleatics** (Cambridge: Cambridge University Press, 1948).

but a measurable edge. For the Greeks the circle is a plane and the problem that was of interest was that of bringing it into a commensurable condition. Thus the squaring of the circle became for the classical intellect the supreme problem of the finite. So a profound problem for Greek mathematics was to alter surfaces bounded by curved lines, without change of magnitude, into rectangles, and so render them measurable. When one looks at this in regard to sculpture and artistic expression of form-feeling, there is always a supreme effort to give the dancing or wrestling forms the pose and attitude in which surfaces and contours have all attained proportion and meaning.[89]

The Greek mathematicians use the word *soma* for their entities, just as Greek lawyers use it for persons as distinct from things: *somata kai pragmata*; *personae et res*. Spengler argues that in classical number the integral and corporeal inevitably seek to relate themselves with the birth of bodily man, the *soma*. The number 1 is thought of as the beginning, the prime stuff, *arche*, of the number sequence; the origin of all true numbers, and thus of all magnitudes, measures and materiality. In the group of the Pythagoreans its figured sign was also the symbol of the womb. It is 2 which is the first true number, which doubles the 1, and which was correlated with the male symbol and given the sign of the phallus. On Spengler's interpretation, 3, the holy number of the Pythagoreans, was symbolic of the act of union of man and woman, even an erotic suggestion in the mathematical operations, namely that of number generating, a suggestion that in adding and multiplying, the processes of increasing and propagating useful to classical man, can be easily seen. The domain of the Apollonian is the near and small. Classical geometry concerns itself with small manageable figures and bodies, and remained unaware of the difficulties of establishing figures of astronomical dimensions, which in many cases are simply not amenable to Euclidean geometry.

In her study of the essence of Greek art, Gertrud Kantorowicz analyses what she coins as the in-the-body-movement for the Polykleitan canon, developing her reflections through a direct visual study of the Doryphoros. Her analysis has important implications for the understanding of the relation of the body and movement, how one grasps what is essential in the Greek conception.[90]

In examining the Doryphoros and the Diadoumenos she observes that the two tendencies of the upright body are played off in the 'purest opposition'. The opposites of the pull of the ground and the striving away from it, heavy and light, of things that grow or are inert, is represented so that the two tendencies are being shown as independent and intact alongside each other.

Polykleitos grasps that the body in its upright position points upwards and has the power to feel independent, free of the solid ground. Thus he gives everything over to free play, relaxed muscles, with neither pressure nor weight; there is a suggestion of an effortless swinging out of freed-up body contours. But this co-exists with another law, namely that the body weighs down; it cannot dispense with the ground, which both supports and draws it down. The forces of the body stream out in opposite directions, 'seeking their appropriate pole'. The streaming forces meet each other in their push to ascend and descend, and they turn back, or rather, there is a turning.

Unlike in Egyptian art, the body does not turn into a weighty cube. As she later notes, the body in Egyptian art is subject to a much more geometric constraint, or a geometric principle, where structure, surface and outline of the body are determinable on the basis of abstract planes and lines: 'the whole figure is like a powerful cube and resembles an architectural pier. That for example is why the joints cannot be elaborated, their narrowing contraction cannot be attended to because that detracts from the cubic principle of composition'.

What determines these bodies has little or nothing to do with them. Whereas in the Greek conception 'the body itself is the controlling factor'. The essence is indeed to grow upwards and to be rooted below, to be bound to the earth and yet free, to be a creature of both place and movement, and it is its inherent nature thus characterised that is the criterion of its formation.

The movement which is 'negated' is not frozen up, or rigidified; rather, the upward and downward forces meet at the centre of the figure, they coil there like a wound-up spring, a rest such as in the tension of a snake about to strike. The movement does not point beyond the body; it remains embodied, that is, it is as 'in-the-body-movement'. This latter term translates Kantorowicz' term *einverleibte Bewegung*, which also figures in the text, not as the perfect participle used as an adjective but as the present participle, *einverleibende Bewegung*.

In the foreword to the text, Benson indicates that Kantorowicz draws on the concept of Georg Simmel to explain what is at issue here; referring to Simmel's idea of 'life', she says:

[I]t is the essence of Simmel's idea of 'life' to revert (while always remaining in flux), to turn against itself, to 'transcend itself'. It may thus be represented by the symbol of a circle of movement regressing into itself, of self-contained, living infinity. But in this lies a profound affinity, beyond all difference, with the Greek world, whose enigmatic wealth – namely the revelation of life being, the fixation of becoming in perfect form – has been missed, over and over again, only because the modern period has not been able to grasp, with its shattered concepts, a dynamics which becomes formed into a pattern that, while growing, rests in itself.[91]

It is this metamorphosis of the forces of movement to rest which constitutes the 'inner intentionality of contraposto'. Kantorowicz adds that this is particularly discernible in Polykleitos, whose personality lent itself to the most clear and simple, the most nakedly evident presentation of the way the Greeks experienced their own corporeality.

It is perhaps only Merleau-Ponty's conception of 'the flesh of the world' that allows us to

89 O. Spengler, **Der Untergang des Abendlandes**, in two volumes, vol. I, 1918, and vol. II, 1922. I have drawn on the first volume.
90 Gertrud Kantorowicz, **The Inner Nature of Greek Art**, trans. J.L. Benson (New York: Caratzas, 1992).
91 Ibid., p.14.

[1]

[2]

[3]

[4]

1 Doryphoros of Polykleitos, after reconstruction from statue of third quarter of 5th century BC. Bronze.
2 Egyptian statue of Saboere with a figure personifying the province of Koptos. Metropolitan Museum of Modern Art, New York.
3 Statue of Ti, 198cm high. Egyptian Museum, Cairo.
4 Diskobolus of Myron, copy from statue of mid 5th century BC. Marble.

appreciate the distinctions which Kantorowicz draws. The calmly erect bodily stance of the surviving statues of Polykleitos contain a movement which simply fulfils the inborn tendencies of growth and weight, which arise out of the constitution of the human body itself, 'and have to work as polarities out of sheer necessity'. This is different to how we understand movement. How did the Greek portray 'real' movement? Kantorowicz examines the motifs of movement which are captured in the work of Myron. Looking at his Diskobolos and Marsyas, one has the instant that most effectively conjures up relentless action.

Through a concrete examination of what is seen in the phenomenon, Kantorowicz says that the point of the arrangement – the structure of crossing and naturally balanced diagonals, the chiastic principle of composition, exemplified in the backward twist of the upper body connecting sharply with the forward movement of the right leg, the contour of which, if continued, cuts sharply across the oblique axis of the torso, which in turn is picked up by the trailing left lower leg, continuing and completing the contrast, or the second pair of complementary opposites, the throwing arm which has its immediate continuation in the right upper leg – achieves the same quality of retro-current, reversible, negated movement brought to rest in a closed circuit, where the body is not coerced into a space beyond it, but left within its own limits. In fact it creates these limits and integrates the body into itself, the stream of the forces is always on the move, clearly definable impulses are released on their course, each one of which makes contact with its counterpart and is stopped, but the impetus then must retrace its course, which it does 'only to be met again at the center of the moving body by its counterforce, whereupon the process takes place all over again'.[92]

Movement is a component of the very essence of the statue, and Kantorowicz argues it was this need to absorb movement into sculpture that marks the work of Polykleitos and Myron. What is achieved in the work of Myron is a brilliantly simplified theorem of equilibrium, or understood in terms of dynamical statics, a principle of indifference. It is the moment of the recoil of the pendulum, the swing that becomes the counter-swing. The figure is equally committed to both movements. Thus Myron's achievement is the conquest of movement. This is the discovery of recurrent, negated, 'in-the-body movement'.

For Kantorowicz this belongs to the body as body in the world. Turning to consider the figures of the wrestling group from the west pediment of the temple of Zeus at Olympia, she remarks how one is shown at once in flight and seizure, yanking and grabbing, parry and thrust, all of this driving towards the centre of the pediment. The group is stationary nevertheless, because it is composed around a central point. This is marked by the head of the centaur. His huge body indicates the counter-direction. It is the weighty mass and central position of the centaur that holds the other bodies in balance. Despite the intermingling of the bodies, they complement and support each other. 'Not only in that the figures counter-thrust each other, but

92 Ibid., p.33.

each one is within itself held up and held back just as the whole group'. No other art than the Greek knows or has created any such necessity as this raging containment of struggle, or this unconstrained constraint, the untied tying together of the group.[93] Kantorowicz is aware that the movement which she is calling typically Greek, since it stands in opposition to modern conceptions and definition, is described as a paradoxical unity of incompatible contradictions, viz. as stationary self-negation, as moving stability, as reversed flowing, oscillating stance, accelerating standstill, balance of uncontrolled passions catapulting to the goal line, and as self-enclosed figures. All of this is then subsumed, she acknowledges, into one concept: 'in-the-body movement'. Grasping this paradoxical principle of movement in Greek art, 'is to grasp the human being who has presented himself in it'.

Kantorowicz holds, even considering the violence of the Olympia figures, that it clarifies one principle: 'equipoise in Greek art in no way implies a reduction of the impacting energies'. It requires a detailed phenomenological analysis to complement the insights of Kantorowicz and to grasp her central conceptual innovation. Clearly the body is not considered here as a perceiving thing in some form of spatial container. In one sense we can say her analysis is to study the join of the body and world, and to analyse the crossing thresholds in terms of their reversibility, turning, and the chiasmic.

The question that needs further consideration in trying to understand the validity of this principle of equipoise is how such unrestrained movement was to be made to function in the austere tectonic framework of the Doric temple by means of such a self-regulating tectonic dynamics of the group itself.

Thanks to the researches of Max Raphael it is possible to address this question directly, as he too sought to understand the notion of the classical body from investigation of the central figure in the west pediment of the temple of Zeus at Olympia, and insisted that at the heart of this art is dialectics, which is fundamentally inimitable. One of the supreme ironies of history, he says, is that such a dialectical art should come to be regarded as the most dogmatic, 'as the mother of all academisms'.[94]

If we examine the figure, we see that like the pediment it is most closely related to the architecture, and within the pediment it is closely related to other figures. This suggests a relation as part of a community and a 'formal whole'.

As would be expected, given the formal difficulty attached to pediments populated with relief figures, the triangular space imposed by the tectonics of the roof involved difficulties for the sculptor, as it is impossible to show characters of the same dimension in a triangular frame whose height progressively varies. One solution was to vary the module. An example of this, rare and fairly extreme, can be seen in the apotropaic Gorgon figure of the Temple of Artemis at Corfu, probably early 6th century, where the menacingly striding figure of the

Gorgon is accompanied by a visibly diminished figure of Chrysaor, and smaller figures fill in at the angles.

Another solution was to vary the attitude. Thus figures could be shown in various attitudes, kneeling, crouching, recumbent, standing. This 'method' can be seen in the early Siphnian Treasury at Delphi (around 525 BC) in the Temple of the Alkmaionids, and the Megarian treasury at Olympia. Greek artists rapidly and through trial and error found solutions which then rapidly established themselves as conventions, and in this case the quest for verisimilitude, the striving towards the 'the greatest possible similarity between image and reality', led to the abandoning of the shifted or varied module as at Corfu, and the search was on for better pictorial responses to the architectural constraints.

So, as the metope favours subjects with two or three actors, and the continuous frieze favours many groups, for pediments with the necessity of showing people lying and kneeling, battle scenes became popular, although not obligatory.

If there were constraints in the triangular pediment, there was also an invitation. The triangular frame of the pediment has an axis well marked by the line bisecting it from the upper angle and dividing it into two symmetrical wings. The Greek term for pediment is *aetos*, eagle, and suggests outstretched wings. However, it was not *de rigeur* to follow this geometry. Examples which tell against this can be found on the small archaic pediments on the Acropolis at Athens, such as the Olive tree pediment. Nor was there symmetry in the Old Man of the Sea pediment, with Hercules battling a Triton on the left, and on the right a three-headed monster with triple serpentine tail watching the fight.

However, there is no necessary correlation between accommodating different heights and iconographic homogeneity. The concern for such iconographic homogeneity can be disassociated from a concern for axial symmetry and symmetrical organisation.

Uncertainty ended about methods of responding to the pre-imposed restraint of architecture in the early 5th century. The definitive formula was adopted in 480 BC at the Temple of Aegina, and twenty years later, at the Temple of Zeus in Olympia.

In the east pediment a variety of attitudes is exploited, 'that is perfectly adapted to the axiality and symmetry of the tympanal triangle'. The central figure of Zeus is shown with slightly smaller humans near to him: Pelops and Oinomaos, the *comes*, the fiancee of one man and the wife of another, then the *quadrigiae*, and lying in the angles the personification of two local rivers, the Alpheios and Kladeos. The personified rivers are watching the episode of the transfer of royal status from Oinomaos to Pelops. In principle the Greeks showed their gods anthropomorphically. On the west pediment the battle of the Lapith and the centaurs is composed in the same way. The scene is dominated by the axial figure of Apollo.

The varying height of the pedimented area only partly determines the choice and arrange-

93 Ibid., p.38.

94 I have in this section of Raphael directly translated from his **Temple, Kirchen und Figuren** (Frankfurt: Surhkamp, 1989). See my: 'Max Raphael, Dialectics and Greek Art', in **Footprint**, DSD Journal, no 1, 2007. For current research on the discussion of Raphael on materials and techniques, see: **Greek Sculpture: Function, Materials, Techniques in the Archaic and Classical Periods**, ed. Olga Palagia (Cambridge: Cambridge University Press, 2006), and bibliographies.

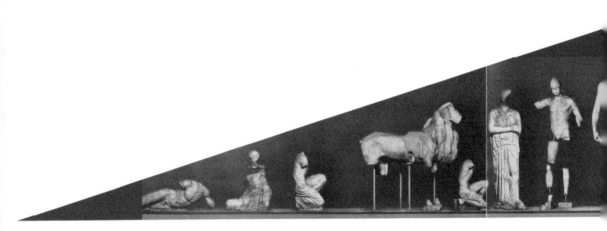

Complete overview of east [upper] and west
[lower] pediments, Temple of Zeus.
After Ashmole.

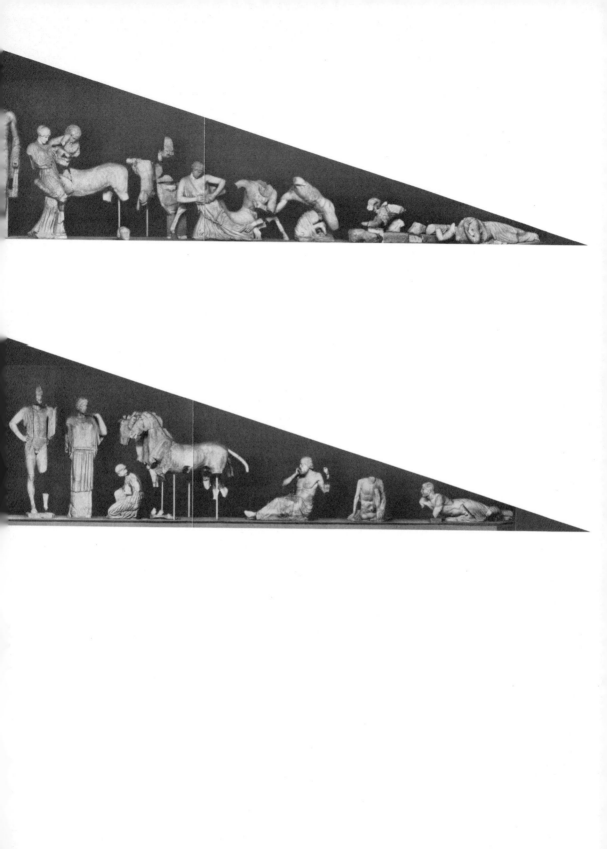

[1]

[2]

[3]

[4]

[5]

[6]

[7]

[8]

Kneeling youth, east pediment, Temple of
Zeus.
Kneeling youth (Myrtilos?), east pediment,
Temple of Zeus.
Kneeling girl, east pediment, Temple of
Zeus.
Seated boy, perhaps Arkas, east pediment,
Temple of Zeus.
River-god (Kladeos or Alpheios), east
pediment, Temple of Zeus.
Lapith youth, west pediment, Temple of
Zeus.
Lapith girl, west pediment, Temple of
Zeus.
Seer, perhaps Lamos, east pediment,
Temple of Zeus.

[1]

[2]

[3]

[4]

[5]

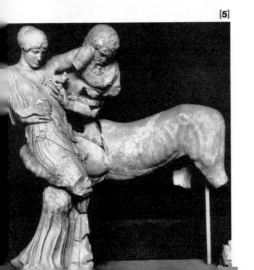

1 Centaur and Lapith youth, west pediment, Temple of Zeus.

2 Figure of Apollo, west pediment, Temple of Zeus.

3 Theseus and Centaur, west pediment, Temple of Zeus.

4 Lapith youth, Centaur and Lapith girl, west pediment, Temple of Zeus.

5 Deidameia and the centaur Eurytion, west pediment, Temple of Zeus.

ment of the objects presented in it; its shallow depth determines the type of modelling, which in this case is in high relief.

In his study of Greek temple architecture, Max Raphael argues that the varying height of the pediment, which increases as one moves from the sides to the centre, imposes a distinction between main and secondary figures, and a gradation in the importance of the action, and even a specific manner of regulating this action.

The strongly accentuated centre imposes a symmetrical arrangement and precludes a continuous development from a beginning to an end, and since the slanting sides of the triangle suggest a rising movement if they are seen from both ends, and a falling movement if they are seen from the apex, the dimension of width is broken up into two opposed directions, and this is what raises the problem of their unity. Similar problems arise in the dimension of height.

The form of the pediment compels the artist to decide not only whether each of his figures can suggest a rising or falling movement, but as to how each of them should embody both movements in its own way.

In the dimension of depth the figure, the human figure, is situated between the open space in front, with its light and air, and the impenetrable wall behind, so that the volume of the body can be developed only in parallel and diagonal directions in relation to its two different boundaries. Raphael makes the telling observation that the outstretched arm and the head of the figure suggest the form of a half pediment, thus the form of the pediment has been introduced into the human figure. Conversely, the asymmetry of this figure has been carried into the symmetrical form of the pediment.

The height of the pediment at mid-point, that is, the height of the pedimental triangle, performs two functions: it co-ordinates all symmetrically located elements, and it introduces a paradoxical asymmetry at the point of convergence. There is then a double function, one of centring and one of breaking-up.

From this Raphael draws an important interpretative key, that there is an emotional effect in this contrast, which is further strengthened by the fact that the pediment rests securely on the entablature. However, the tallest and significant central figure in the pediment is not supported by a column, but stands above a void which opens into a dimension of non-being.

However, it must be noted that the middle axis of the edifice is at first purely ideal, and remains intangible and invisible in the central intercolumniation. It is only in the triglyph that it is framed by an architectonic form. Only in the pediment does it achieve plastic form. At the very point where the ideal axis achieves physical existence it is broken and shifted. Instead of the previous apparent perfect symmetry, there is a balancing of the similar and symmetrical, but uneven, masses around an axis. This is a fluid balance. It is a synthesis of actual imbalance and ideal balance.

In his study of the Doric temple, Raphael had drawn attention to the significance of the ideal triangle for the temple of Paestum, where it touches the lower corners of the abacus in the two central columns, which is so important for the static play of forces, while in the corner columns it touches the upper corner of the abacus, so that the contraction of the intercolumniation of the façade is closely related to the height of the abacus, and the phenomenon of contraction and tapering becomes recognisable as two variations of the same idea. The real pedimental triangle that crowns the temple façade is thus just the combination of the ideal triangle in the dimension of height and dimension of depth and related to the space, the perpendicular forces of load and support, and the proportions.

The two slanting sides of the pediment suggest two movements, one rising from the corners to the centre, the other falling from the centre to the corners. This is also matched in the peristyle by the fact that the spacing between the columns is greater at the centre than at the sides.

The greatest height and the heaviest part of the pediment is above the widest intercolumniation, the point of weakest support. If we disregard this structural paradox, which seems resolved in the pediment by the linking of perpendicular forces with the horizontal thrust, it remains that the two movements, along the columns and ideally on the horizontal, continue in the peristyle. They are not, however, related internally.

In contrast to this, the simultaneous centripetal and centrifugal movements in the pediment are effected along two slanting lines, which are so to speak the parallelograms of directions. They are the results of two vectors, horizontal and vertical. Thus, their function is one of mediation.

The triangle begun in the peristyle is completed in the pediment, nevertheless, it only remains a part. It is a part not only of the actual front, but also of the ideal rectangle, whose diagonals we can obtain by extending the sides of the pedimental triangle. The actual triangle becomes part of the enveloping ideal space, that is, not embodied in material form, just as the space surrounding the structure, below the pediment, remains invisible. The basic attitude to infinite space is expressed in the dimension of depth and height.

The intention is to limit the space physically, to express only a part of the whole, but at the same time to express the whole in the part. The slanting lines of the pediments are the result of two forces, not just of two vectors. The upward thrusting force, the support, is gradually dematerialised with the tapering of the columns. The down-thrusting force, the load, is increasingly materialised in order to hold back underground powers in the horizontal stairs. The pediment mediates between the two forces. It should not be looked upon as a static frame, but as a field of opposing forces, which has become form. The Greek temple embodies and is the embodiment of the dialectical interaction of antithetical forces of various kinds, spatial, physical and intellectual. Architecture here embodies such forces in a permanent, finite, harmonious and clearly articulated structural body.

Raphael had first developed that conception in his work on the Doric temple, but staying with his analysis of the elements relevant to the form of the pediment sculpture, it is clear that the most important element of this is the depth of the pediment.

This reference to depth refers to the intrinsically small interval between the open space in front and the pediment wall behind. The sculptor is guided in his treatment of this space in the same way as the architect applies his treatment to the space between the stereobate and the cella wall.

Standing in front of the middle axis of the temple, we see the two centre columns almost frontally, the next two at an angle, and the two corner columns at a sharper angle. The columns never stand exactly in the axes of the plinths, and thus the lights on them are distributed asymmetrically. This creates a great variety of light, ranging from brilliance to darkness. This is further enriched by the varied light and dark areas inside. Lights and shadows of various intensity and quality play on the surface on all sides.

The conception of the Greek architect starts from an ideal structure closed on all sides. This is transformed into actual artistic structure by: 1) opening the ideal wall to admit surrounding air and light, so that an air-filled space is placed in front of the space encompassed by the building; 2) opening the part behind this air-filled space at several points and creating an alternation of masses and voids and a vibration of the void around an axial plane; 3) indicating a diagonal which runs from the corners of the steps and through the corner columns, cutting across all the parallel planes on both sides to the centre, and 4) leaving one solid wall which checks the play of masses and lights, only to open up behind it the inner spaces.

It is the same principle of alternating air-filled spaces and portions of the wall and diagonal intersections which is applied by the sculptor in his treatment of the space of the pediment.

The argument for unity is further enhanced by the consideration of the column and showing that it was created because the architect felt the need to break up the ideal wall, and to express the contrast between the full and the void as a stage in the process of opening up depth Raphael suggests a thought experiment which helps to visualise the operation of the centripetal and centrifugal forces in the cross-section and the elevation, if we imagine that the opened wall has been rotated around its axis to produce a cylinder.

This accounts for the flutings; the outward surface of the cylinder is drawn inward in relatively wide grooves and sharply pushed outward in narrow ridges. The original surface of the cylinder is broken up into many actual surfaces of contrasting curvatures, and one imaginary surface parallel to the original curvature, formed by the ridges.

Ridges and grooves run along the entire column in unbroken straight lines. These rigid rational geometric lines constitute as it were the outer aspect, of the activity and mechanical forces

[1]

[2]

[3]

[4]

1 Figure of Pelops, east pediment, Temple of Zeus.
2 Figure of Zeus, east pediment, Temple of Zeus.
3 Figure of Oinomaos, east pediment, Temple of Zeus.
4 Figure of Hippodameia (or Sterope), east pediment, Temple of Zeus.

between centre and periphery. They enable us to view the column as a complex of forces that are tied together visible at its neck, in order then to open up of their own accord and 'to spend themselves'.

The form of the echinus can be read as a reversal of that of the shaft. The Greek column is not compelled to support, but does so, as it were of its own accord. Although the column originates in space-forming forces that have nothing to do with the perpendicular static forces of load and support, it is a form that not only provides support, 'but is also in perfect balance with all the other forces, so that developing energy and actual structure constitute an indissoluble unity'. What Raphael shows is that, just as the column was developed from the ideal wall, so the human figure was developed from the shallow space of the pediment in accordance with two principles, that of the supporting and relaxed leg, and that of rotation. These principles are combined with the boundaries of the block in a three-dimensional system of co-ordinates that is shifted in several directions.

The starting points are different; the architect starts from the spurious infinity of physical space which he transforms into a finite spatial body that contains the true infinite. The sculptor starts from the finiteness of the physical body and tries to express in it the infinity of the totality of the spiritual and artistic space. The two paths cross and complement each other in a single reality whose material surface is the unity of all developed oppositions. Both sculptor and architect use the same method.

Here we can understand the body more clearly. According to this theory the mechanical play of forces in the objective world is analogous to the play of ideas in consciousness; subject and object, being and consciousness are in accord, or coincide through the mediation of the human body. It is the human body which, once thinking and being have been conceived as distinct entities and have entered into a sufficiently close relationship, can become the vehicle of the synthesis of both, because the human body shares in both.

In this conception of what is an epistemological problem, mechanism and organism cease to be an absolute antithesis, and mechanism, within certain limits, can be treated artistically in analogy to the organism, as an organism can be treated in analogy to mechanical forces.

The consequences for architecture which Raphael draws from this are the following: firstly, the entablature is placed like a continuous horizontal band on the individual vertical columns, and since no column is directly connected with the one next to it, it is the whole row of columns that supports the entablature. Secondly, the round echinus and the square abacus are fitted to each other as closely as possible. This is very much in contrast to the tall blocks on the top of Egyptian columns. Thirdly, each of the two elements influences the form of the other: the weight of the entablature is expressed in the column by the enstasis, and the rising movement of the column is expressed in the triglyph above the abacus. The difference between the two influences is shown in the triglyphs, which seem to be flowing downwards, and is stressed by the guttae.

The presence of a homogeneous chain of supporting forms, the mediating function of the capital, and the influence of each formal element on the other distinguish the treatment of the perpendicular forces in the Doric temple from that of any other architectural order.

It should be noted that the treatment of forces varies according to whether or not they come into contact with full masses or a void. Such variations reflect the original opposition between the full and the void. Further variations occur in the treatment of these oppositions. The full is rendered in the squat form of the echinus or the abacus, which does not yield to pressure and embodies the pure zero point. The void is rendered either in the narrow dividing line between the echinus and the abacus, or in the shadows which envelop the entire capital.

It is a result of the type of interpenetration between the full and the void that grants the predominantly dramatic, or lyrical, one can even say, epic character to the temple. These differences depend on the line of vision of the viewer and varies with it. There can be no schematic interpretation because of this issue of visibility of the perpendicular forces, for example of the sculpture.

The body is related not only to the architecture but also to other human figures in the pediment. They together form a meaningful and coherent unity. The mirror-like symmetry between the two halves of the pediment serves to stress the contrasts between the struggling parties and between moments of dramatic suspense and moments of activity. This makes it finally clear, in a point that fully adumbrates the observations of Kantorowicz, why asymmetries within the over-all symmetrical order are so important here. For, it is only by means of asymmetries and contrapostos that movements in time can be expressed in static terms. But, only those asymmetries and contrapostos are artistically justified which serve to express differences with respect to time, stages of development, or intensity. Otherwise they degenerate and become mechanical, as Raphael suggests they often do in Renaissance art. For example in the two figure groups the asymmetries play an even clearer role than in the single figure composition, one group of which faces towards the centre whether placed on the right or left, whereas the other faces away. This indicates clearly that the two triads on either side of the pediment are separated by a time gap. Failure to recognise the dialectical play of time and space exemplified in the sculptural work leads inevitably to the pseudo-classical contraposto and the academic 'organ-pipe' arrangement.

The relation between whole and part is not one of direct dependence. The whole does not directly determine the parts. This absence of dependence and direction is made possible by the operation of a formal mathematical principle which governs the geometrical shape and the proportions of the whole and the part, so that their harmony is achieved independently and each preserves an appearance of freedom.

Its mathematical character shows that it was conceived as a link between the Idea and the Phenomenon. The order to which the conflicting forces aspire was an order of being. The whole was always conceived as an articulated whole, which was not allowed to impinge on the independence or freedom of the part, no more than were the parts allowed to break up the whole. The proportions that governed the parts were adjusted to the proportions that governed the whole, as elements of the latter. The absolute dimensions of the elements determined the proportions.

From the whole a unit of measurement was derived by a series of operations and the unit of measurement led back to the whole in a series of operations in reverse. Therefore the community of elements in the Doric temple cannot be expanded, the temple is a finite whole, incapable of any metaphysical approximation to the infinite.

A further series of observations on the axial system is in place, and helps to grasp what is essential for classical art all the way down to the deployment of particular techniques. It is this which gives Raphael's analysis such power that it can help one understand the finite body of the architecture both in its making and as process. The axial system in its relation to the original block plays a prominent part. Each axis introduces a specific orientation into the undifferentiated body of the block, and this results in a separation which sorts out one direction from the other and opposes it to them so that the block is built around the axes.

Each axis reduces one of the planes of the block to a line and finally all the lines to a point, so that the two operations can be carried out in every dimension in two directions, and further the directions can be said to converge or diverge.

This leads to a two-fold process, depending on whether we view it from within or without; that is to say, the block is reduced from planes to lines to a point, or *vice versa*, the point can be expanded into space. Space is transformed into an active process with this shifting of the axial system. The key question here is: what is the cause of this shift which results in a figure characterised by subjection to space and freedom to determine space? An understanding of classical art depends then primarily on the relationship obtaining between figure and space, or to state it more precisely, on man's relation to space as defined by his stance.

The three elements which signify diversity in the figure analyses from the Olympia pediment are extension-flexion, raising-lowering and rotation-counter-rotation. The supporting leg suggests that it has not been disturbed by an outside force, but is tied to the ground and capable of providing support. The relaxed leg suggests it has been disturbed, and is detached from the ground and thus incapable of providing support. Here there is a simultaneous and differing effect of a cause, which is shown by different reactions as observed by the artist. The supporting leg is capable of providing support only because it is itself supported by a firm and resistant body. This body can only be the earth. This is what gives it the strength that caused the other leg to bend. The resulting flexion creates an angle, which with the angle of the arm opened out in the opposite direction creates also alternating convexities and concavities. These recur in rounded forms at the edge of the drapery, on the opposite side of the figure, where they clearly suggest waves.

In that sense earth is opposed to water. But apart from that interpretation, there is the fact that we have one leg bound and held by the earth and the forces of the earth, and beside it a leg that is about to move, that contains all possible movements, but does not move, that is a merely potential movement not followed by an actual movement.

It is this mobility, both momentary and permanent, that makes the flexed leg incapable of providing support. Thus, load and support within the human body, the statics of its perpendicular forces, is dependent upon forces that transcend the individual body.

The classical position of the legs has been interpreted as a reduction of the Egyptian walking position, but one is more justified in deriving the movement of rotation from the dancing step. The new stance could be interpreted as a synthesis between two ritual movements, running and dancing. The new synthesis is based on the comparison of complete finitude of stationary point with the infinity of open space. The stance embodies the elements of initial disturbance, resistance, restored balance, potential and actual movement, and an unsupported load floating in space.

The play of the perpendicular forces is also only part of a greater interplay, whether interpreted as disturbance and restoration of balance, or as freedom and un-freedom. Even though the function of the perpendicular forces is thus restricted, it is of fundamental importance because it humanises conflicting extra-human forces and resolves the conflict between them on a human plane.

Differently from the articulation in archaic art of the stones' masses as determined exclusively by the proportions and forms of the human body, classical art conceives of the human body as a complicated play of self-regulating levers, each acting upon others and reacting to them, and action and reaction are always balanced in accordance with the principle of the organic muscle. The classical body is a machine constructed after the pattern of the living organism, and muscular action is suggested even where the position of the masses could be accounted for by gravitation alone.

The axial system provides an over-all frame for the figure and its parts, which links the universal and the concrete, idea and forms. This is the biune cause. The biune cause is the key to an understanding of the classical conception of man, just as cosmic-mystical monism is the key to understanding the Indian dualism and that of the Egyptian, and triunity that of the Christian conception.

It is the human figure which fully embodies the operation of the biune cause which shifted the axial system. The question then is, how did the artist embody the unity between the inner and outer world in matter as such? This requires a precise material analysis.

One can begin by examining the question of perception. Light penetrates into the marble, animates it without dematerialising it. Classical art is bound to marble to such an extent that one could say that without marble it would not exist. No other art has ever used marble for the same purpose or treated it in the same way as classical art.

Marble is harder than poros and softer than granite, as an artistic medium it lies halfway between poros and granite. Raphael draws on the writing of Richard Lepsius to better account for the material features of marble. Marble is metamorphosed limestone, the result of a gradual recrystallisation of the original carbonate of lime. That is why in nature one finds all transitional forms between dense, shelly limestone and granular crystalline marble. Limestone is composed of very tiny formless and structureless semi-transparent grains of carbonate of lime, often with admixtures of ferriferous substances, of which a sufficient amount can give the limestone a black or dark grey colour. Marble, on the other hand, is composed of relatively large crystals of calcite; the structureless particles of chalk and the dark-coloured carbonates have disappeared, the former having been transformed and combined into larger crystals of calcite, and the latter combined with oxygen to form carbonic acid. In some varieties of marble, for instance Attic marble, only a part of the rock has been re-crystallised, and a certain amount of semi-transparent grey chalk particles is found among the large calcite crystals.

Other varieties of marble are completely crystallised and coarse-grained, but because of the presence of other mineral ingredients, the mass is not translucid, but milky white, dark grey or even black, and light can penetrate it only to a small extent. A lower and older stratum of Attic marble, Pentelic marble, is clearly stratified. It is snow white and of a somewhat dull milky colour, with a suggestion of yellow. It clearly shows its crystalline structure, and is composed of a very large number of small calcite crystals, whose cleavage planes display sparkling facets in strong light more luminous and shining.

Parian marble is even more bright. It was used in the pediment sculpture of the temple of Zeus at Olympia, and differs from Attic marble by its coarser grain. The grains of the calcite are fitted closely together in a mosaic; the size of the crystals rarely exceeds 3 mm. In the purest variety of Parian marble, *lychnites lithos*, the average size of the crystals is 1-1.5 mm, occasionally 2-3 mm.

Because of its coarser and firmer crystalline structure, lychnite is more transparent than any other variety of marble, and light penetrates it for a greater distance: 35 mm as against 15 mm in Pentelic marble. It is this relatively deep penetration of light that largely accounts for the beauty of good Parian marble. It is very hard, i.e. firmly structured and the individual grains are strongly knit together. It is thus less affected by exposure to air and this too accounts for its transparent glow. Lychnite has no stratifications, the crystals of calcite are never arranged in rows, but irregularly dispersed in the rocky mass, so that the effect is one of compactness.

From this description by Lepsius, Raphael notes two natural properties are emphasised, the fact that light can penetrate the marble, and that it is structured even in its natural state. In the physical aspect of his creative method the artist too takes these facts into account in the technical treatment of the medium.

The tremendous blocks used for the Olympia pediments were first prepared with a hand drill consisting of a sharply pointed iron shaft, which was revolved by the palms of the hand. For finer work, which can be divided into three stages, the main tools were the point, or pointing chisel, and the tooth chisel, or claw tool.

The point can be placed perpendicularly to the block of marble and vigorously hammered into it, or placed at an angle and hammered carefully, so that a long groove requires frequent interruptions. The first method sometimes results in crushing the crystals, which can diminish or even destroy the glow of the marble and produce ugly white spots.

What remains critical in the handling of the marble is the recognition that the close union of the inner and outer is captured in the light penetrating it. The discovery that light penetrated the marble probably inspired the idea of centring the modelling around a plane parallel to the surface; the curved forms move towards the light, and as a result the light becomes inseparable from form.

For the viewer who first scans the stone, his discovery, guided by intuition, is that light and air coming from the surrounding physical world penetrates the medium and makes it come alive. The stone cutter has created a homogeneous surface by using the point to remove a layer of rock before resorting to finer tools which were not used until all the parts of the statue were carved out.

The latter point supports the proposition that it is the essence of classical art to represent the individual idea not so much through the human figure, but *as* the human figure. Even in the argument with regard to the light and form it is necessary to understand that it is closely related to the conception of an air-filled space. It differs from the Egyptian conception of juxtaposing full and empty areas in the block and endowing both with equal intensity, and it also differs from the conception of absolutely empty space in which, or in front of which, things are placed. The void is regarded as mere appearance; matter is known as of two kinds with different qualities, and the qualities of air and stone are linked when each penetrates the other, and internally when bodies occupy air-filled space, giving it as it were a spiritual-material quality, while the air dematerialises the bodies.

In this way sculpture is linked to the space outside it, and its distance from the viewer becomes an element of the work and is given form like the other elements. This is why a Greek sculpture seldom looked into the void; it gazes directly or indirectly at the viewer. We can then say that the classical artist recognises that ideality and reality are opposites, and that he accepts this opposition as an absolute necessity. He does not spiritualise matter nor conceive of it as a metaphysical substance, he does not conceive the process of creation as a gradual descent from ideality to materiality, or as a gradual ascent from materiality to ideality. He achieves the union of the two without blurring their antithetical character, so that each preserves its own specificity. The two are equally important and they form a union in which materiality has become ideal without ceasing to be material, and ideality has become material without ceasing to be ideal.

Ideality is potential materiality just as materiality is potential ideality. The self-realisation of this biunity implies that the potential materiality of the ideal and the potential ideality of the material have been realised.

The two processes lead to a point where materialised ideality and idealised materiality become identical, and this identity is the *gestalt* of the process, the being of the method.

In classical art the objectively given and the subjectively posited coincide without losing their specificity, there is no pantheistic-mystical fusion of the opposites into a sameness, rather each preserves its separate existence, and the two find their unity in man, in the idea of his consciousness which is at the same time the surface of his body. The mode of reality embodied in classical art can be called the 'self-constituting form of material ideality'.

What is the kind of man suggested by the figure? Its physical appearance is largely determined by proportions; for example, the unit of measurement is clearly indicated in the head and feet. The minor difference between the dimensions stresses the importance of their relationship for the overall figuration, *Gestaltbildung*. The fact that the part of the body which is least free and the part which is freest are linked in their inner composition denotes that everything outside the body is related to the body, is made inherent in the body.

The unit of measurement and its subdivisions, one half and one third, remain effective as a measure throughout the figure, but they are rarely exact, and least of all at the most emphasised places. Everywhere there is slight deviance from the fundamental unit, and as a result the metric structure has a rhythmic quality combining necessity and freedom.

In this structure, next to deviations from the exact unit of measurement, combinations consisting of multiples of the unit and with added halves or thirds play a special part. To overlook the difference between metric structure and rhythm, or to imprison the composition in mathematically exact grid lines, would be to reduce the creative process to a lifeless mechanism.

The Greek artists did not feel compelled to adhere to an exact or single rigorous system of proportions, which is clear from the complicated structure, for example, of choruses in classical Greek tragedy which is so different from that of the dialogue.

To the proportions that determine the interrelationships between individual forms and harmonise them with one another, one must add the internal proportions of these forms themselves.

No part of the body is overly contracted at one place or overly extended at another, and nowhere is the continuity between two parts broken or in an exaggerated way stressed. The strongly in-drawn hips, for example, which characterise the archaic type of human being is eliminated, and the shoulders are no longer considerably broader than the hips. Bones are emphasised when this is justified by their function, e.g. knees, hips, shoulders, so that the body appears as a solid structure. Elsewhere the bones are surrounded by flesh in such a way that bones seem to attract the flesh, incite a cleaving, and hold it firmly, and the flesh seems to loosen the bone. The simultaneous effect of tightness and looseness rests no doubt on the treatment of the muscles, which are fully adequate to their function; the part they play is not overstressed and it gives a strong impression of spontaneity.

The mechanical functions involved in the living interplay of the parts of the body are clearly shown, yet they are fully integrated into the whole, precisely because each part performs many functions, spatial, measuring, static, compositional, which relativise one another, and because the artist's imagination is concentrated on the reality of the form as a whole. We are shown changing tensions and relaxations, that is, there are slight quantitative variations in the unit of energy and volume because energy no longer serves magical purposes when it always has to be at its greatest intensity in order to ensure success in attack or defence. Rather, it is conceived of as the living force of the human body, expressing the interplay between action and reaction, which leaves no room for absolute inertia or absolute energy. More than that, the power of the body stands for the power of the spirit, is completely identical with it, whereas in Egyptian art the power of the body testifies to the magic of rebirth.

So, the figure stands within the block whose greatest height, without the head, equals six and whose width at the hips equals one-and-a-half, or two with drapery. Between the shoulders and the hips the torso forms a rectangle within the rectangle of the block. Then the width decreases considerably, the lower part of the body even seems narrower than it is because the area occupied by the two feet seems reduced by being in the shadow.

The entire lower body could be inscribed into an angle, parallel to the frontal plane, and with its apex located between the feet; if its sides were extended to the arm-pits they would abut against the rectangle of the torso.

The resultant figure links the centre of the bottom side of the block with the corners of its top side, and consists of a rectangle placed above a triangle. Sensibility is more closely associated with the body than any other psychic faculty. Man is essentially a sensory being, he perceives the world with the whole surface of his body, and his nervous system is open and receptive to all stimuli.

In classical man sensibility is neither dominated by irrational emotions, nor rationalised by understanding. It is expressed as a balance between man's physical and spiritual forces. It is love for the world as a whole, not for specific material objects, nor the metaphysical Idea of Ideas.

This sensibility is not passive receptivity, for the *sensorium* is faced with a force which prevents man from becoming the product of his environment. This force does not merely react to stimuli, but is spontaneous and capable of initiative. The *sensorium* has as its counterpart a *motorium* which stimulates action as such rather than action in response to outside stimuli. The balance between sensorium and motorium is not brought about directly, but through the mediation of consciousness, which set limits to both, thus achieving not only external balance but internal unity.

Classical man stands then in an artistic and philosophical conception of space which is centred around him, concentrated in him, and at the same time extends beyond him. It defines his conflict as human, a conflict that is not created by man, but that is inherent in him and that he cannot elude.

In summary, Raphael's analysis leads to a biune principle, which does not manifest itself as such but by its effects, the opposition between gravity and consciousness, *daimonion ananke*, finitude and formlessness, so that the man represented and the viewer live simultaneously in all dimensions, which meet at a single point. Each of these spatial and spiritual dimensions has its own inner opposite in a form that is both abstract and concrete, potential and actual. These various modes of being, as well as the various dimensions, remain at first separated, one beside the other, but also in the greatest tension with each other, a tension that is measurable by pure intuition. They remain bound to one another and we see no development, no process of emanation.

Just as in the original block all dimensions and directions are both present and absent, so all the modes of being are present and absent at the point where the dimensions and directions intersect. This co-existence is not developed as something objective, but is posited as something subjective, yet in such a way that the positing is immanent in the objective without being able to manifest itself.

However, as will be seen, the Greek inheritance in its cosmological, and Timaean, sense would be developed historically and primarily towards a cosmological and divine meaning. It goes without saying that such thinking is still operative in the world today and of consequence in trying to understand the long *durée* of historical reflection on the model and its architecture.

In his study *Cosmology and Architecture in Premodern Islam*, Samer Akkach suggests his work is a commentary on a quotation from al-Ghazali:

As an architect draws the details of a house in whiteness and then brings it out into existence, according to the drawn exemplar (*nuskha*) so likewise the creator of heaven and earth wrote the master copy from beginning to end in the Preserved Tablet and then brought it into existence according to the written exemplar.[95]

95 Samer Akkach, **Cosmology and Architecture in Premodern Islam** (New York: SUNY Press, 2006), pp.50-53.

In his commentary on this, Akkach wants to capture what he designates as the 'spatial sensibility', where in pre-modern Islam the cosmos is graspable by means of number, geometry and alphabet. There is a structural resonance and a pattern of correspondence which is based on the divine model governing all modes of manifestation and creation.

He identifies as the corner stone of spatial sensibility in pre-modern Islam the deployment of space along three axes, which correspond to the symbolic participation in the cosmic and metaphysical order from the architectural order. We can trace later how this culminates in the neo-Pythagorean relation of the body and cube, in the most sacred monument of Islam.

The chief mystical and hermeneutical source used by Akkach is the work of ibn al-Arabi (b.1165, d.1240), where the divisions between the sensible and the intelligible, the physical and the metaphysical, parallel the relation between the seen and the unseen.

Of the voluminous writing attributed to Muhyi al-Din ibn al-Arabi, known as al-Arabi, and referred to as 'al shayk al akbar', the 'greatest master', the single most important source, because of its importance for subsequent Sufi ontology and cosmology, is the *al-Futûhât* (translated by Chitticks), which is extensively cited in Akkach's ground-breaking study. For al-Arabi, positing the world of the seen and the unseen, considering the forms in a Platonic sense, the world of similitudes or images, *'Alam al-mithâl*, surprises the secrets of being, of which one is the servant, and which one can come to know only in the intimacy of worship.

The pathway to the unseen is through analogy and metaphor. The seen world as the outer shining, the *zâhir*, is readily accessible, imagination has access to the abstract through the mediation of the embodied. In the generation just before al-Arabi, ibn al-Arif, a celebrated Andalusian thinker who died 1141, referred to the power of the symbol for such access, and the enigma of the symbol, a call from a distance, and a negative event, a disclosure of an essential deficiency.

One can argue that for ibn al-Arabi the world is an exact shadow of the absolute manifesting *zill*, at three different levels. At the highest level are the archetypal forms, that is, immutable essences; at the second level of shadow, there are natural beings that project immutable essences in embodied forms, and at the third level of shadows sensible shadows project the silhouette of natural bodies on sensible surfaces. Symbolism helps trace the process of universal man-

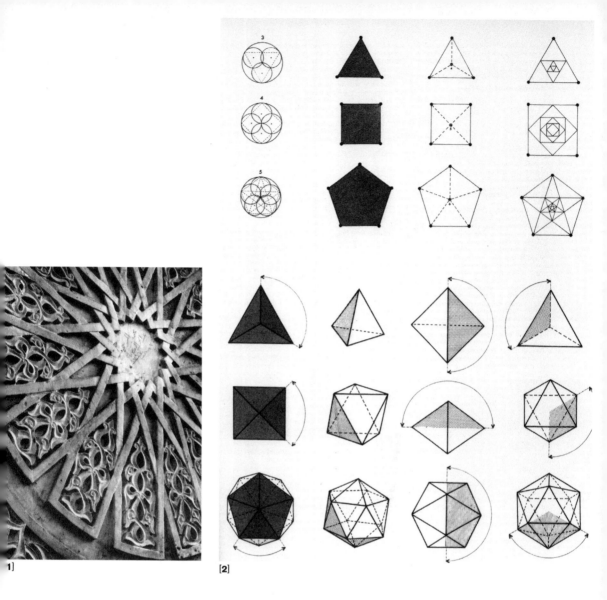

1] Photograph of detailed 16-point star
inside Aqsa Mosque.
2] Pythagorean shapes transforming into
three-dimensional structures according to
Critchlow.

ifestation. Through symbolism one can understand the link, the *vinculum*, by which sensible objects take their final shape through an ontological sequence of differentiation, making it possible to trace a sensible form back to its original source.

This triplex ontology of shadows corresponds to the three-fold mirror of Ficino's developed *Platonic Theology*, and indicates a common source for the work of ibn-Arabi in Greek thinking.

In Ficino, the process also further accounts for the act of human creation, itself a translation of the divine creator. This is most explicitly found in Ficino's *Dell'Amore*, where universal beauty is taught as being the 'splendor of the face of God'. Ficino's metaphor depends heavily on al-Kindi's *De radiis*, itself derivative of neo-Platonic metaphysics:

> The divine power, supreme over the universe, mercifully infuses with his ray, as though they were his sons, the angels and spirits created by Him. This divine ray, in which there is the fecund energy of creation, depicts the order of the entire world, in the Angels as more akin to God, much more clearly than in worldly matter. Hence this picture of the world which we see in its entirety is better expressed in the Angels and in men, than what appears in our eyes.
>
> In the latter he found the shape of all the Spheres, the Sun, the Stars, the Elements, rocks, trees, and animals. In the Angels these images are called ideas and prototypes; in the spirits, reason and knowledge; and in worldly matter, appearances and forms. These images are clear in the world, more clear in the spirit, and clearest in the Angel. Hence one and the same face of God is reflected in three mirrors in order, in the Angel, in the spirit, and in the human body...the splendour and grace of this visage, as it is reflected either in the angel, in the spirit, or in worldly matter, whichever it might be, must be called universal beauty, and the desire that is attracted to it, universal love.[96]

Ficino's philosophy is an invitation to see with the eyes of the soul the soul of things. True to the Platonic thesis 'that the root of every reality is a form', Ficino thought of the movement of knowledge as the process directed from the perceptible impression to the idea that approximates it, not the verbal-conceptual term, but in the rich fluidity of an image that guides the mind to the perception of the supreme light, so that 'all the ornament of this world, which is the third face of God, offers itself incorporeal to the eyes through the light of the incorporeal sun'. The human being is the link or marriage tie of the world. As Garin notes, born as light the universe is converted into love. The texts of Ficino themselves became models.[97]

The long development of the doctrine of rays stems from the writing of al-Kindi. Outside of Ficino's work this has the most impact in Alberti. The dominant metaphor here is that of visual rays. In other words, the visual rays that are depicted in the *reticolato* of Alberti and the array of the surface show that the rays subtly penetrate the air and thin and clear objects, until they strike against something dense and opaque, where according to Alberti they strike with a point and adhere to the mark they make, rays which Alberti imagines to be like 'the finest hairs of the head', or, 'like a bundle tightly bound within the eye', where the sense of sight has its seat. There is an efflorescence in the swaddled bud of the eye which extends its shot rapidly in a straight line on the plane opposite.

In al-Kindi it is in the continuous relationship between composite bodies, planets, that all parts are constituted. Elements, bodies, objects, images, words, musical notes, souls: everything transmits rays. There is a constant procession from all bodies, that is the *vinculum* for all mutual connection. Knowledge of these connections was essential for magicians in practice.

There is a theory of making at the human, natural and divine levels, and the distinction between forms of making, a practical and a theoretical. However there is no distinction between making and designing:

> Practical art is the artificer, the knower, externalising the form that is in his mind and placing it in matter. The artefact is the whole made up of matter and form together. This begins by the influence of the Universal Soul on the process forced by the Universal Intellect with the Order of God – exalted be his praise.[98]

There is however a sequential relation of form to matter which terminates in Prime Matter, *al hayûlâ al-ûlâ*, i.e. simple substance. At the human level, form/matter is reflection of a complex ontological structure and hierarchy. Making is not an exclusively human activity.

There are four different kinds of making which relate to four different kinds of matter. We can speak of making, creation of artefacts, at the human, natural, psychic, and divine levels. At the first level are included shapes, motifs and parts; at the second level, the sensible forms, of animals for example; the third level is related to the Universal Soul and concerned with pattern, *nizam*. At the divine level, the inventor of all inventions out of no-thing, understood as the abstract forms.

The human level involves matter of artificial work, and includes every *jism*, body, be it timber, iron, stone etc and the *jism* is the 'mother' of artificial work. There is a matter of natural work, a universal matter and prime matter. In the divine artefacts there are abstract forms without matter. This is the domain of original identity, or primordial substance, and it precedes all substantial differentiation – it is the intimate state of divine being, and there are simple intelligible forms that cannot be sensed.

96 For comments on this passage see: Eugenio Garin, **Portraits from the Quattrocento**, (New York: Harper and Row, 1972), V, 'Images and Symbols in Marsilio Ficino', pp.142-161.
97 Ernest Gombrich, 'ICONES Symbolicae: The Visual Images in Neo-Platonic Thought', in **Journal of the Warburg and Courtauld Institutes**, 11, 1948.
98 Akkach, **op.cit.**, p.37.

[1]

[2]

1 Interior of the Dome of the Rock.
2 Calligraphic inscriptions on the Dome of
the Rock's upper exterior façade.

However, when original identity, quantity, quality, and the intelligible forms are related to one another, some act as matter while others as form; thus, quality is a form in quality; quantity is matter for quality; quantity is a form in identity, and identity is matter for quantity. Therefore, the archetypal model is of chains of differentiation that establish an unbroken chain, linking human, natural and divine acts of making.

A further distinction is made then between necessary and complementary form. Necessary form includes the foundational qualities of all bodies in space, length, breadth, depth, configuration, movement, light and purity, and complementary form is what gives an object its sensible characteristic. Necessary form here translates *sura muqawwima*, and complementary form translates *sûra mutammima*. It should be noted that the translation of the Platonic *eidos* as *sûra* includes senses of likeness, or similitude, *mithâl, mathal*, as in the expression *Alam al-mithâl*, 'realm of images', 'world of similitudes'. Access to the realms above is through the medium of the body and especially the imagination.

Imagination, *khayâl*, relates to form and matter. Ibn al-Arabi states: 'He who does not know the status of the imagination is completely devoid of knowledge'. The I is bound to the sensory world, there is no power of creation *ex nihilo*. The human creative ability is to synthesise.

Man is active in the intermediary world, and in an image of direct Quranic origin, there are two seas between which there is an isthmus; that is to say, between absolute being and non-being there is a mediator, which is the intermediary domain of archetypes of all possible existents; between the necessary and unrestricted self-existence and the non self-existent this intermediary world is viewed as an isthmus.

The order of universal manifestation contains triplicity and quadratures, and the *isthmus* is the medium through which the delivery of world from potentiality to act is effected. The higher world is the world of unseen, angels, abstract meaning; the lower is the corporeal and seen, and the intermediary realm, the *'Alâm al-khayâl*, combines the bordering worlds, and the spirituality of the unseen is incorporated into the corporeality of the seen to create the subtlety of the imaginary: in sensible matrices the abstract meanings take on bodily forms.

The special power of the imagination is caught nicely in the ringing injunction of this quotation:

Know that you are an imagination and everything that you perceive and of which you would say 'this is not me', is also an imagination. So the whole being is an imagination within an imagination.[99]

The imagination does not, however, escape the world of the archetypes. Imagining, *tasawwur*, and drawing, painting, forming, *taswîr*, all derive from the verbal root *sawwara*, with its mean-

99 Ibid., p.43.

ings of to form, configure, fashion, draw, paint; and in making there is a marriage between the practical, viewed as the father and active, and the intellectual, viewed as the mother and passive, through which forms come into existence. In the intermediary activity the artefact is a 'child' born from this fruitful relationship. The term *sana'a* is primarily 'doing' or 'making'. Even if everything that people make can be viewed as artistic making, nevertheless, calligraphy is nobler than carpentry.

Throughout we still find that artefacts reflect the patterns of divine realities. When a human artefact reflects or corresponds to the qualities of natural artefacts not only would it resonate with the universal order, but also the maker would be measuring his work against the work of divinity.[100]

It is through the divine names that divinity is acquired, and the 99 names are divided into names of essence, actions and attributes. From al-Ghazali we can infer that the human act of building, for example, involves activities similar to the divine act of creating the world. Both involve production of exemplars according to which an object is made. Three actions are required to bring an object into existence from non-existence: designing, *taqdir*, bringing into existence, *ijâd*, and form-giving, *taswîr*. These actions relate to three of the divine names: the name as the creator, *al-khâliq*, the producer, *al-bari*, and form-giver, *al-musawir*. For al-Ghazali these names are not synonymous. It is part of the human lot to share in the name *al-musawwir*, not in *al-khaliq* and *al-bâri*. The architect, *muhandîs*, works in accordance with design and form-giving. This participation allows access to the image of being externalised in the pattern or blueprint of the world, *nuskhat al'âlam*. There is no subject-object dualism in the Sufi account, rather there is a dynamic polarity of presence, which refers to a modality of being with all the realities it entails, the relations it involves and the influence it commands, and absence.

This knowledge is concentrated in numbers and geometry, and the mathematical sciences, which include number, geometry, astronomy and music, which four divisions have the principles of number, unity or number one; geometry, the point, astronomy, the movement of the sun, and music, proportion or equality of two ratios. The foundation of designing is geometry, in which the sensible and the intelligible unite. From the *Ikhwan* the following gnomic observation:

> When in his craft, an artisan designs before commencing work the act involves a kind of intelligible geometry.[101]

The point is the principle of geometry in Sufi teaching, as 1 is the principle of number. Perhaps it is in the text of the *Ikhwan* that we find the most pertinent understanding of the point and line, which demonstrates both its sensible and intelligible modalities in effect, and points to the generative dimension of this geometry; it is also consonant with the taking on of divine character for the human, a begetting within being that is properly creative. It is necessary to quote it *in extenso*:

An intelligible line cannot be seen on its own, but only as it lies between two surfaces, like the borderline between sunlight and shade. If there were no sunlight and no shade you would not have seen a line (defined) by two imaginary points. And if you imagine that one of these two points is moving while the other is standing still, until it returns to where the movement began, a plane will occur in your mind. An intelligible surface, too, cannot be seen on its own, but only as it lies between two bodies, like the common surface between fat and water. An intelligible point, too, cannot be seen on its own, but only where a line is divided by imagination into two halves; wherever a division is indicated the point is marked there. And know, O brother, that if you imagine this point moving in one direction, an imaginary line would occur in your mind. And if you imagine this line moving in a direction other than that toward which the point has moved, an imaginary plane would occur in your mind. And if you imagine this plane moving in another direction to those of the point and line, an imaginary body that has six square planes with right angles, that is, a cube, would occur in your imagination. If the distance to be traced by the movement of the plane is shorter than that traced by the line, a brick-like body (*jism labiniyy*) will occur, and if it is longer, a well-like body (*jism bi'riyy*) will occur, whereas if they are equal, a cube will occur.

And know, O brother, that every straight line conceived in the imagination must have two ends which are its two extremes; they are called the 'two imaginary points', if you imagine that one of the two points has moved, while the other stayed still, until it returns back to the point where movement began, an imaginary circular plane will occur in your mind. The still point then becomes the center of the circle, while the moving point marks in your mind, by its movement the circumference of the circle. Then know that the first plane that occurs is the quarter of the circle, then the third, then one half, then the circle. If you imagine that the curved line, which forms half of the circumference of the circle, is moving while its two ends are still, until it returns to where it began moving, a spherical body will occur in your mind. So it is clear to you, from what we have said, that intelligible geometry is the reflection on the three dimensions, which are the length, the width, and the depth as abstracted from natural bodies.

And know that many of the *muhandisin* (geometers, architects) and scientists imagine that these dimensions, I mean length, width, and depth, have forms that exist by themselves, without knowing that this existence is wither in the substance of the body or the substance of the soul. To the dimensions, these substances are like matter (*hayûlâ*), and in the substances the dimensions are like form (*sura*), detached by the thinking faculty from the sensible bodies. If only they knew that the ultimate aim of studying mathematical sciences is the

100 Ibid., p.49.
101 Ibid., p.57.

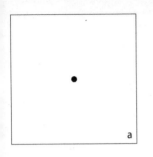

a

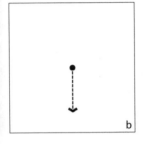

b

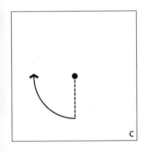

c

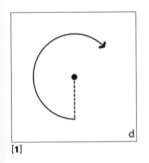

d

[1]

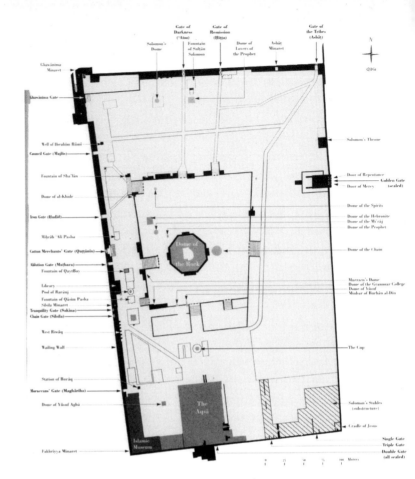

[2]

1 Critchlow's drawings on geometric progression.
2 Site plan: Haram al-Sharîf.

training of the students' souls to be able to abstract, through the senses, the forms of the sensible bodies and to conceive their essences by the intellectual faculty, so that when the sensible bodies disappear from contact with the senses these forms – which have been transmitted from the imagination to the intellectual faculty, and from the intellectual faculty to the memory – remain formed in the substance of the soul. The soul, then, when turning to itself will dispense with using the senses in perceiving the information. It will find the forms of all information in its own substance.[102]

The differentiation of the created world occurs in modalities, and being takes on different levels of manifestation. In the account of Akkach, Islamic architecture has a discernible preference for geometrically ordered spaces with isotropic spatial qualities. Further, he notes there was a tendency to organise spaces symmetrically around a central point. This is true of both secular and religious buildings, namely that symmetrical elements are recurrent in a wide variety of building types, e.g. the formal composition of a dome on a geometrically regular base, or a courtyard with a central fountain and four vaulted doorways.

This is what Akkach understands as spatial sensibility, which is graspable through the sense of ordering and spatial structure it reveals. The elusive connotation he evokes with this term allows him to apply a broad comparative analysis among diverse geographical and historical periods, building types and regional variations. Spatial order is understood as individual spaces that are pictorially and experientially unified.[103] Even where compositional qualities may vary widely, as in the Taj Mahal in Agra, Masjid-I Shah in Isfahan, the Dome of the Rock in Jerusalem, the Sultan Hasan school in Cairo and the courtyard gardens of Alhambra, 'the same sense of spatial ordering is clearly visible in all'.[104] The varieties of design and tectonic expression reveal two types of composition: concentric and linear, although it should be noted that the linear composition is a variation on the concentric composition, which includes repetition, examples of which can be seen in pre-modern bazaars, such as at Isfahan, Kashan, Aleppo and Jerusalem.

By concentric is understood architectural designs that are laid out about a stationary centre, exemplified by two models: a centralised enclosed space and a centralised open courtyard. The best examples of this, where a roof emphasises unity and the base emphasises directionality and spatial deployment are the Dome of the Rock and the Ashrafiyya school in Jerusalem. A centralised enclosed space develops from a regular polygon, usually quadrangular, and expands from a focal point and evolves symmetrically about a central axis.

The simplest architectural 'embodiment of this model is a building with a cubical base and a hemispherical dome'. The composition of the Islamic mausoleum follows this model, and even though they vary greatly in shape and scale most of them are composed of a geometrically regu-

102 The text of this quotation can be found at Akkach, **op.cit.**, pp.159-161; it is based on the edition of **Ikwan al-Safa, Al-Risala al-Jamia**, ed. M. Ghalib (Beirut, Dar al Andalus, 1984), Ras, 1, 102.
103 Akkach, **op.cit.**, p.151.
104 Ibid., p.151.

lar base with a domical or conical roof, and internally reveal the same order. This can be seen in the Cities of the Dead in Cairo or the Gunbads in Iran, which Akkach views as variations on a theme, since they exhibit the same spatial regularity and symmetry, although in the case of the mausoleums in tower form, for example the Gunbad-I Qabus or Gunbad-I Ghazan, they emphasise the vertical axis.[105]

Internal courtyards can form part of buildings such as mosques, schools, houses, and on a larger scale a garden or the central space of an entire city. Whether the determining model of a large complex or only part of it, the centralised courtyards expresses the underlying order of the concentric composition. Islamic gardens follow this model; this is especially true of large gardens in the Iranian plateau and India. The planning of some early cities such as al-Kufa, al-Basra and Baghdad also follow the model of a centralised open courtyard.

A key feature of linear composition is the repetition of the spatial unit, 'creating a number of individual concentric spaces or spatial pulses'.[106] The linear manifests a multitude of centres all of which are equally important. Nodal points, such as intersecting routes, or an entry being emphasised, break the monotony of the linear.

The concentric composition is the basis from which the linear derives, 'just as the point is thought of as the principle from which the line extends and stillness as the state from which motion proceeds'.

The significance of the relation of the architectural order to the cosmological and metaphysical order can be seen in considering the first house, the cube of the Ka'ba. One can compare the thinking around the conception of a divine model for the first house, and the way in which the house of the Prophet functions as a model in the development of mosque architecture.

The conception of a divine model realised in the Ka'ba is traced by scholars from within a rich tradition of sources and discussion. The notion of a sacred space and how it is chosen still remains unclear. That spaces as the manifestation through difference of divine unity were given differential weight and value, with spaces being designated the efficacious, more efficacious, or most efficacious, is clear from the sources. Akkach doubts the application of the highly influential work of Eliade and Otto for the evidence he considers; the thesis of Otto in his remarkably influential work *Das Heilige* of 1917 where the holy designates the mysterious, the numinous, the irrational, indeed the main framework for defining the holy, was a perceived conflict between the rational and the non-rational.

105 Ibid., pp.154-5.
106 Ibid., p.158.

[1]

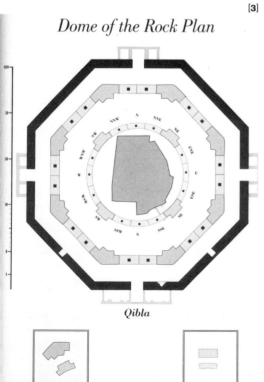

[2]

[3]

Dome of the Rock Plan

Qibla

PIERS

SPANDRELS

1 City of the Dead, Cairo, Egypt.
Aerial image of the north cemetery.
2 City of the Dead, Cairo, Egypt.
Aerial image of the south cemetery.
3 Dome of the Rock Plan.

Islamic patterns and their geometric properties.

Otto's thesis being that the holy is the completely 'other', which is echoed in Eliade's claim that the sacred is the opposite of the profane, and the sacred breaks into non-differentiated *continuum* of the profane, creating rupture; with the manifestation occurring space becomes centralised and time cyclical, or as Akkach has it: 'the amorphous becomes structured according to archetypal paradigms'.[107]

Eliade's theoretical work was enormously influential and the sacred-profane polarity was quickly exported via a functionalist interpretation into architectural discourse. It was easy to define a split between religious and secular architecture; a prayer hall because of its use relates to the holy, for example, but not a bazaar.

The problem as Akkach sees it is that the notion of the profane as translated into Arabic, as *al-âdî*, the ordinary, or *al-mudannas*, the 'impure', desecrated, does not imply the polarity suggested by Eliade in his interpretation of mythico-symbolic functions and spatio-temporal conditions, and he notes that a 'sacred' without a profane is conceptually different from a 'sacred' with a profane, preferring to see a process of preference indicated in the mainly panegyric term *fada 'il*, meaning 'merits', 'virtues' or 'excellencies'.

The development and pervasiveness of the *fadâ 'il* discourse developed laudatory geo-mythical conceptions, which allowed the construction of imaginative geographies that differentiated sharply between places and blurred the boundary between the mythical and the real: 'it is through blurring of spatiality that *fadâ 'il* confers significance on places, buildings, and landscapes. The way things are materialises divine preference'. For Akkach the logic of divine preference hinges on the necessity of difference. Difference was predicated on a preference, a divine preference, and the *fadâ 'il* conception is an attempt to lay out spatially a matrix of such differentiation and exhibit the pattern of divine partiality, or 'a literary act to inscribe the ontological foundation of difference'.[108] It is clear of course that inscription is itself a distinct spatial practice.

The horizon of reference for difference is Islam. As might be expected in such a complex relational field, the interconnections are established within the connection themselves, and the act of orientation becomes existentially decisive as when one considers the desire of the Prophet to orient his prayer in another direction than Jerusalem. The new sacred centre, *qibla*, desired by the prophet, was to be the Kaʿba. This is the divinely chosen centre of the Islamic world. The Quranic text reads: 'We have seen the turning of your face to heaven. We shall therefore make you turn towards a *qibla* that pleases you. So turn your face towards the Holy Mosque, and you – O Muslims – wherever you may be, turn your faces towards it (*Quran*, 2:144).

Orientation takes on cosmic significance; it is not just that one faces the Kaʿba, but also there is a directing of the mind towards the heavenly archetypes that lie above. However, the cosmic geometry is still rooted in the orientation that sees in the sun the extremities of spatial orientation as directions, East, West, North and South. The primal condition of sky and earth are held

107 Akkach, **op. cit.**, p.163. For supporting material, see: Jonathan Z. Smith, **Map is not Territory**, chapter four, 'The Wobbling Pivot', and his detailed consideration of Eliade (Chicago: The University of Chicago Press, 1978).
108 Akkach, **op. cit.**, p.167.

in the orientation of the human during the times of his or her orientation to the divine. This fourfold of cardinal directions is also a temporal node of cycles, the four seasons, and of temporal measure, that is, the year, the month, the week, the day. Once again, as in the understanding of the creative mirroring of the creature, a metaphor of binding and generation enters: the spatial and temporal orientations, in their unfolding, are married in the motions of the solar orb.

What is granted by the sun is the regions of appearance, the sun in its diurnal and annual journeys. In architecture one witnesses the marking and re-inscription of these spatial inter-relations, which is a tracing of celestial geometry. The tracing is not by literal transcription, but is the searching of correspondences from the solar cycles, so that Akkach can say: 'the plan of a building becomes so to speak, an architectural crystallization of temporal cycles, a cosmic graph, a projection of celestial geometry, a geometrization of time, and a coagulation of time in spatial form.'

The orientation is also dependent on the temporal activity of the praying human, and the direction and times which are required in this duty. This is the duty of prayer, and the orientation towards Mecca is the orientation to the *omphalos*, the navel and centre of the world. There, to the Ka'ba, God's first house of worship, according to the tradition, Adam was helped by angels to build the primordial house (*al-bayt al'atiq*), which was removed during the deluge. The site was rediscovered later by Abraham who, with the help of his son Ishmael, obeyed the injunction sent from God through a speaking cloud, *al-sakina*, which was that Abraham was commanded 'to build according to the measure of my shadow'. Abraham, it is said, traced the form of a cloud and with the help of his son rebuilt the house as he was instructed: 'And when Abraham and Ishmael were raising the foundations of the house, Abraham prayed: Our Lord, accept this from us, you are the Hearer, the Knower' (*Quran*, 2:127).

This orientation is also a reflexive disclosure of the being of man; by orienting to the centre and obeying the imperative of *al-sakina*, there is centrality and peace; this is the 'peace of reassurance' that has been sent into the heart of the believers, and it obliges dwelling with a quality of stillness that designates the centre *par excellence*. The Ka'ba embodies the world, is the heart of the world, the house of stillness, a centre of peace, and the divine immanent in world. Thus, built form becomes a part of divine geography.

From the research of Frishman and Khan, Hellinbrand, Nasr, and Akkach, one can consider the opposite movement of divinisation of a model and arche-

Drawings of retractable domes for
extensions to the Prophet's Holy Mosqu

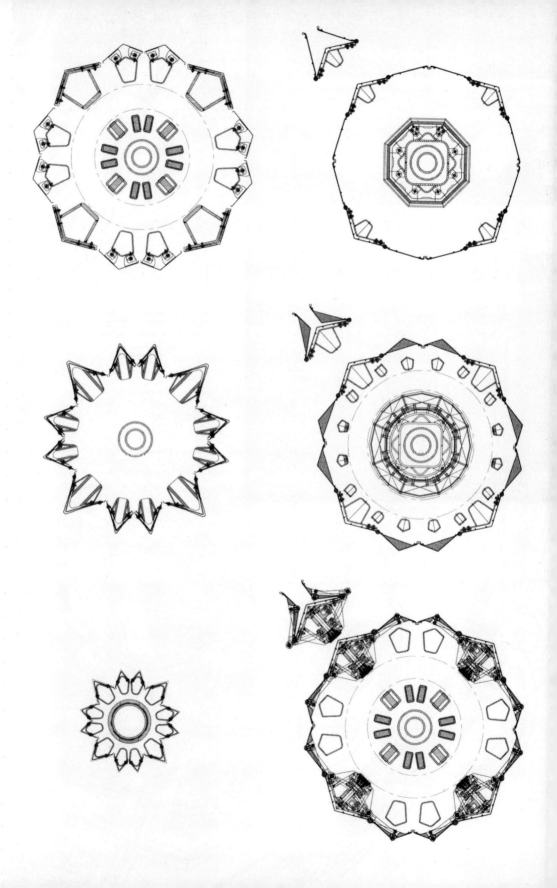

type in the concrete reality of the house of the Prophet. This Prophetic model, being that of a simple dwelling, historically located, and the hypostyle mosque constructed by the Prophet in Medina, served as model that in turn assumed the status of a divinely sanctioned model, irrespective of adaptations.[109]

The complex role of the model can be seen at play in the sources and subsequent developments. One narrative tells that the house of the Prophet was built where his camel al-Quasisa was divinely led to crouch, and another that it was built in the form of an *arish*, like that of Moses, indicating that the Prophet has a model in mind. The reference to the *arish* of Moses suggests a trellis structure, something erected for providing shade, a roof of a building, a tent-like structure.

The house-mosque of the Prophet consisted of a square measuring one hundred or seventy cubits a side and contained two parts, one a simple wall courtyard and the other a simple shelter built with a flat roof, held up by tree trunks used as pillars. The initial building was taken down and reoriented to Mecca a few months after the first construction, which had been built on the North side facing Jerusalem.

The sheltered prayer-hall opened onto the courtyard, the later being the predominant part of the mosque and provided with three doors, on the east, west and north sides of the square.

The most dramatic way in which subsequent development demonstrates how the house became itself a sanctioned model, is the Ummayad Mosque of Damascus, which scholars have argued was the first to reproduce the Prophet's House, or model, at a monumental scale, revealing similar planning and spatial characteristics. This is the model that the house built.

As indicated earlier, the fusion of the thinking of al-Kindi and the Neo-Platonic theology of Ficino can be found within Renaissance practice, and it is to this we can turn to examine further thinking about the model in different historical periods. Vasari, who is a principal source, sets the work of Florence against the Byzantine-Islamic influx of Venice, the city without a classical past.

Much of the most detailed scholarship on the model, historically, is focused on the period known as the Renaissance. In his work, Alberti provides a reference and effective starting point. From his reflections driven by his theoretical concerns we have not only an account of the advantage of the use of the model, but also the manner in which it can be deployed. Effectively it becomes an experimental intervention in which many of the problems for the realisation of the architectural idea can be controlled and guided. It also functions as a form of 'modest proposal' or a restraint on ambition, allowing one to have a clearer idea of the design and convey facts from the side of the architect, that is, act as an effective communication medium, which is achieved through restraint and simplicity.[110] Alberti holds that complexity in the model which advertises the model maker's skill over the architect's communication of the idea, should be avoided. He further contends that models allow the relationality of site and surroundings to be demonstrated. They are instruments for achieving the elusive goal of *concinnitas*, where through the interrelation of number, outline and position, the 'fourth' element of beauty can be given to appearance.

In his Second book, which deals with materials, we find an anecdote that mobilises Alberti's reflection. It is taken from Suetonius's life of Caesar, and relates to the destruction of a house which he had overseen from its foundations, and with a finickety and fastidious disdain, when built, he had it demolished. Alberti takes it that Caesar would have benefited from the following advice, advice which points to where we can find direct and sometimes detailed consideration of the role of the scale model in design practice and the expansion of the uses to which the model is put:

> For this reason I will always recommend the time honoured custom practised by the best builders, of preparing not only drawings and sketches, but also, models of wood or any other material.[111]

Alberti spells out what the benefit and advantage of using such models is:

> These models will enable us to weigh up repeatedly and examine with the advice of experts, the work as a whole and individual dimensions of all the parts, and before continuing any further, to estimate the likely trouble and expense … Having constructed these models, it will be possible to examine clearly and consider thoroughly the relationship between the site and the surrounding district, the shape of the area and the number and order of the parts of a building, the appearance of the walls, the strength of the covering, and in short the design and construction of all the elements discussed in the previous book. … The model (small scale) will allow one to increase or decrease the size of the elements freely…to exchange them and to make new proposals and alterations until everything fits together well and meets with approval. Furthermore, it will provide a surer indication of likely costs – which is not unimportant – by allowing one to calculate the width and height of individual elements, their thickness, number, extent, form, appearance, and quality, according to their importance and the workmanship they require.
>
> In this way it is possible to form a clearer and more certain idea of the design and quantity of columns, capitals, bases, cornices, pediments, revetment, flooring, statues, and everything else relating to the construction of the building and its ornamentation.

The real value of the model is predictive, something to which Alberti often returns:

109 For this see the various publications of Martin Frishman and Hassan-Udin Khan, eds., **The Mosque** (London: Thames and Hudson, 1994), and bibliography. Hossein Seyyed Nasr, **Introduction to Islamic Cosmological Doctrine** (London: Thames and Hudson, revised edition, 1978).
110 Alberti, **On the Art of Building in Ten Books** (MIT Press, 1988)
111 Ibid., p.33.

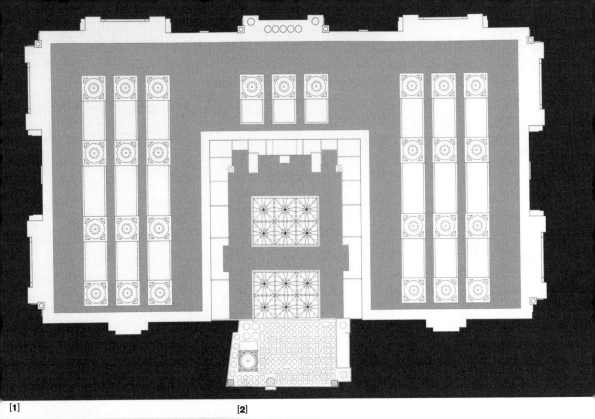

[1]

[2]

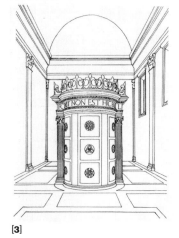

[3]

1 Plan of The Prophet's Holy Mosque, after Serageldin.
2 Children of Mercury, attributed to George Pencz, c. 1530. Woodcut, 298 × 206 mm. British Museum.
3 The Rucellai Chapel, Florence.

…it is advisable to construct small scale models of this kind, and to inspect and re-examine them time and time again, both on your own and with others, so thoroughly that there is little or nothing within the work whose identity, nature, likely position and size, and prospective use you do not grasp… When examining the model, these are some of the considerations to be taken into account. First nothing should be attempted that lies beyond human capacity, nor anything undertaken that might immediately come into conflict with nature. For so great is nature's strength that, although on some occasion some huge obstacles may obstruct her, or some barrier divert her, she will always overcome and destroy any opposition or impediment, and any stubbornness, as it were, displayed against her, will eventually be overthrown by her continual and persistent onslaught. We ought to be careful then, to avoid any undertaking that is not in complete accordance with the laws of nature.

This advice becomes even more particular as if the danger of transgression from the ultimate model was constantly haunting the design process, and so he enjoins practitioners:

I urge you again and again, before embarking on the work, to weigh up the whole matter on your own and discuss it with experienced advisors. Using scale models examine every part of your proposal two, three, four, seven, up to ten times, taking breaks in between, until from the very roots to the uppermost tile, there is nothing concealed or open, large or small, for which you have not thought out, resolved and determined thoroughly and at length, the most handsome and effective position, order and number.

Alberti's treatise is datable as the first in which the model is defined as a clear representation of the idea, and as a place holder for marking the development of a project, which acts as a constant means of checking the process itself. In that sense, it is like an auto- regulating experiment for the design thinking, which responds to the demands of the representation of the idea, and also makes available this thinking to others. The model also needs to be presented, as the quotations show, *nudos et semplices*, naked and simple. There is a stern warning against over-elaboration of the model:

There is a particular relevant consideration that I feel should be mentioned here: the presentation of models that have been colored and lewdly dressed with the allurement of painting is the mark of no architect's intent on conveying the facts; rather it is that of a conceited one, striving to attract and seduce the eye of the beholder, and to divert his attention from a proper examination of the parts to be considered, towards the admiration of himself. Better than that the models are not accurately finished, refined and highly decorated, but plain and

[1]

[2]

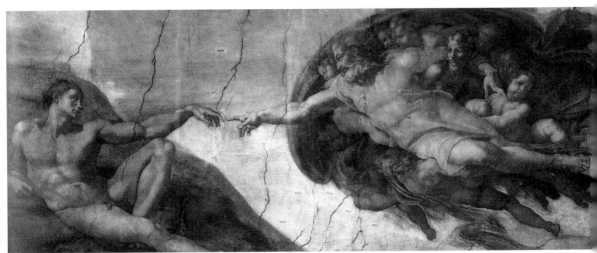

[3]

1 Studies for the lantern of the Dome of Milan. Codex Atlanticus, fol. 266r.
2 Style of Giuseppe Arcimboldo, 'Art man' in service of the Emperor, c. 1580. Windsor Royal Collection.
3 Michelangelo, God Creating Adam, Sistine Chapel, 15th Century. Vatican City, Rome.

simple, so that they demonstrate the ingenuity of him who conceived the idea and not the skill of the one who fabricated the model.[112]

The use of paint and colour is referred to by Vasari, for example in the case of Giotto, and the Albertian emphasis is probably helpful in understanding why there is often a lack of detail, for example in the model-making of Brunelleschi's conceptual artefact, in the sense that its role is one of experimentation and ultimately of abstraction. The model is not in a strict relation to a graphic system of representation, as with the Vitruvian notion of the *modulus*, but acts more as a constructed system of trial and error, which allows some pre-establishing of costs and constant re-checking of the ideas. Perspective ultimately dis-embodies, even as it organises.

In one sense, it is the issue of measure which dominates the consideration of the model, and Sardo also sees this as an echo of Albertian concerns in the treatise of Filarete, where the checking of elements of light and shade, positioning and the relations, allows through the model more and more a measure of control, and a control of measure. Such concerns, which are designated as the Albertian legacy, can be seen again in the treatises of Filarete, Serlio, and especially Philibert de l'Orme who dedicates three chapters of his treatise to the topic of models. Of course his arguments, whilst citing Alberti, also notes that faulty construction is often a result of good or sufficient models. He directly cites Alberti and insists on the clarity and simplicity of the idea of the architect as the regulator of the making of the model, and this serves to express the proportions and dimensions of the building. There is a need to make different models at different scales, as the smaller models with a wealth of detail, often objects of great value, are the most liable to create illusion. This is the feature of the 'thinking mechanism' that is the Albertian model, which Albert Smith also emphasises in his analysis of the Albertian use of the model.[113]

The emphasis on *nudos* and *semplices* is indeed a warning against the illusionistic power of the small-scale model. If the architect is to experiment and play with ideas through the small-scale model, the deepest risk is that this leads to a sleight-of-hand illusionism. It is really only in constant re-checking and in communication with others that one can define the grounds of such an illusion. In one sense, this element is that talking becomes an important instrument in the actual design process, something which modern offices deploy increasingly in order even to minimise the costs of repeated model-making. It is also the importation of a method into design practice. The pressure goes back to the architect and his idea, the clarity of defining the problem at the beginning, and having this guided by the aim of achieving through the elements of composition that ineluctable element of the kind of interactive and sensitive unity that the living face exhibits, in which a *concinnitas* shows itself as beauty.

As already noted, there is often a reflexive loop in the theoretical treatises, where the previous texts themselves become a 'model' to be followed. One can trace a direct filiation from Alberti,

---

112 **Ibid**., p.35.
113 This discussion on the theoretical treatises can be followed in: Sardo, **La figurazione plastica dell'architettura**, see note 18; and Albert Smith, **Architectural Model as Machine** (London: Elsevier, 2004).

through De L'Orme, Scamozzi, and for the English-language evidence the most significant treatise is indeed the publication of Henry Wotton, *The Elements of Architecture*, published in London in 1624. The preoccupation with the economic regulation that can be indicated in the model is of some interest and indeed Wotton provides a specific consideration of that most professional of users of the model in the Renaissance, Sangallo.[114]

The complex overlaps that emerge have been well expressed by Chastel in delineating the interleaving of three different aspects which characterise the fragmented state of Italy, which became not only a Europe in miniature but itself the 'atelier of Europe'. He speaks of an epigraphic and archaeological humanism with its principal centre in the North, Padua, a philological and philosophical humanism which develops in Florence, and a mathematical humanism with its main foyer being Urbino. In reality all these aspects mingled and were interwoven together, sometimes in fantastic syncretisms, where disciplinary interest and practice were often fused or simply jostled together in a strange medley. Foucault has pointed to this in relation to Renaissance science and the ways in which different analogies are used throughout different but interrelated discourse.

Indeed if one turns to the 'Life of Alberti' supplied by Vasari, the tone is one of dignified but distant respect, even a cursory read casts doubt on how much the theoretical and practical could meet in a character such as Alberti's, who Vasari rather reproves more than once for the over-theoretical character of his work.[115] The suggestion is that, when he really took the trouble, he could create something exceptional but was often guilty of lapses. Thus Vasari praises the service offered to Sigismondo Malatesta, of Rimini, for whom he designed the church of San Francesco, notably its marble façade. Vasari considers it one of the foremost churches in Italy. When the Rucellai wanted to build in marble the façade of Santa Maria Novella, Alberti was consulted, and he gave not only advice but supplied a model. The façade was finished in 1477, and people were delighted with the door; 'It is clear that Alberti took exceptional trouble over this project'. However when it came to the work of Cosimo Rucellai, in the Loggia opposite the palace in the street called La Vigna, and in the House of the Rucellai family in the Via della Scala, Alberti showed in the first instance a lack of judgment and design in the way he tried to vault the interior: demonstrating very clearly that theoretical knowledge must be accompanied by experience; no-one can develop perfect judgement unless his learning is tempered by

114 All this can be followed in Sardo, **op. cit.**, chapter 4.

THE
ELEMENTS
OF
ARCHITECTVRE,
Collected by
HENRY WOTTON Knight,
from the beſt Authors
and Exam-
ples.

LONDON
Printed by IOHN BILL,
M.DC.XXIV.

[1]   [2]

Title page of 'The Five Orders of Architec-
re' by Vincent Scamozzi.
Title page of Henry Wotton Knight's
he Elements of Architecture.

practical application, whereas in the second case he used the correct and true method as it was employed in the ancient world. Again in his criticism of the Servite church of the Annunziata in Florence, 'built after Alberti's plans and model', Vasari suggests that Alberti would not have made such an ingenious and difficult structure if his practical experience of architecture had matched his theoretical knowledge.

Many of the designs and models of Alberti were used by Fancelli (Luca) the Florentine architect and sculptor. Vasari remarks that it is useful for architects to have friends who were willing and able to serve him thus, 'because architects cannot always stand over their work and it is a great help if they can find someone to execute it faithfully and lovingly, and I (if anyone) know the truth of this from personal experience'. In the case of his collaboration with Bernardo Rossellino, Alberti, during the pontificate of Nicholas v, became the *consiliero dei consilieri*, the advisor of the papal advisor, and contributed to the restoration of the ruined aqueduct of the Acqu Vergine fountain and to the construction of the Trevi fountain.

Vasari is clearly citing Vitruvius in his strictures on the combination of the theoretical and the practical, but in the main no such fine balance was easily achieved, at time the practices of the workshops were themselves the main reason for new practice and media. Alberti's theoretical developments of perspective would be tried and tested in workshops, leading to new and different applications such as in the vogue for *intarsia* tables with perspective arranged scenes.

The new position of the architect as an intellectual is clearly important in the work of Vasari, himself an architect. However Sardo, echoing the thesis of Goldthwaite, emphasises in his study that the real source of innovation and the changing status of the model can be found in the workshop practices, for example of the gold-makers' guild.

In accounting for the model, no source is more directly helpful than that the *Vite* of Giorgio Vasari, architect and almost single-handed inventor of the monograph on the artist, which whilst still echoing the hagiographical tradition of the Middle Ages, clearly replaces miracles with the skill of the craftsman, and introduces the concept of *maraviglia*, wonder, the marvellous, miracle, at the 'divine genius' which flourished through the Florentine renewal of the arts, which he places most squarely in a tradition begun by Cimabue and Giotto, breaking with the Byzantine tradition and culminating in his living contemporary, the supremely inspired genius Michelangelo, for whom Vasari expresses admiration verging on idolatry.

In the Preface to the *Lives*, Vasari takes design to be the 'animating principle of all creative process'. God who is the Divine Architect, in time and nature, in his perfection showed how to create by a process of removing from and adding to material. Subtraction and addition then are the primary processes for creating, in the way that good sculptors do, and painters who 'by adding and taking away ... bring their rough models and sketches to the final perfection for which they are striving'. The *vis-à-vis* of the analogy is telling. In his quest for a genealogy of the arts, Vasari, allowing for the problems of chronology and the uncertainty regarding the antiquity of the Ethiopians and Chaldeans, believes that the origin of the arts was nature itself, and that the first image or model 'was the beautiful fabric of the world'.

Within his own account of the origins Vasari also registers a subtle shift away from nature to the work of the artist himself, a shift which his own writings model and begin to install as the primary form in which the work-as-life is communicated. We can trace this in how he positions Cimabue and Giotto. Whilst Cimabue was on Vasari's account adopting some of the draughts-manship and 'method of modern times' – that is, he was moving away from the Byzantine style and also shed light on and opened the way to invention, including his act of expressing the meaning of his painting with the help of words – it was nevertheless Giotto who would himself become a model that painters were always striving to imitate and reproduce.

The shift to the artist's production and the notion of reproduction enter Vasari's account and place the artist's process of creation in the front line of consideration. The break with the Byzantine style – and ultimately Vasari is also raising the stakes for Florentine pre-eminence against Venice – is characterised vividly and allows one also to understand what the 'modern' style consisted of: it moved completely away from the Byzantine unbroken outline, staring eyes, feet on tiptoe, sharp hands, absence of shadow, 'and other Byzantine absurdities'. What Giotto achieves is graceful heads, delicate colouring, animation in the heads, more realistic folds in the depiction of drapery, and even a contribution to the art of foreshortening. Importantly, he was the first to express the emotions of fear, hate, love, anger. There is also the subtending theme of verisimilitude, with Vasari emphasising in the Giotto biography that he was drawing from life at an early age. Drawing and *disegno* were fatal companions in Vasari.

For his work in architecture he records that on July 9th, 1334, Giotto set his hand to the Campanile of Santa Maria del Fiore. The details of the laying of the foundation of solid stone at a depth of about forty feet, after the water and gravel had been excavated, on which a box was then laid of about twenty-four feet of good ballast and the remaining sixteen feet laid with masonry, also added weight to a later claim, found in the Preface to Part Two of the *Lives*, that architecture had its most pregnant renewal in Arnolfo and Giotto and made reasonable progress, and Vasari adds: 'they improved proportions of their buildings, making them not only stable but in some measure ornate'.[116] The work carried out was according to the original German style, and 'Giotto designed all the subjects for the ornamentation, very carefully marking the model with white, black and red colours where the marble and the friezes were to go'. Drawing on the writing of Lorenzo di Cionene Ghiberti, Vasari also believes that Giotto was responsible not

115 I have used Vasari, **Lives of the Artists**, translated and selected by George Bull (London: Penguin Classics, 2 volumes, reprint, 1987).
116 Vasari, **op. cit.**, vol.I, p.86.

[1]

[2]

[3]

[4]

1 Filippo Brunelleschi, model for the lanter
of the Dome of Florence, 15th century.
2 Filippo Brunelleschi, a model for the
Dome in Florence, 15th century.
3 Antonio da Sangallo il Giovane, internal
view of model for the project of the Basilica
of St Peter in Rome, 1539-1546.
4 Bernardo Buontalenti, model of the façade
for St Maria Del Fiore, 16th century.

only for the model of the Campanile, but also for some of the screens in marble which are the beginning of the arts of sculpture and relief. Lorenzo claimed to have seen models in relief from the hand of Giotto, and in particular, Vasari notes, for the works mentioned above.

This confirms a second move in Vasari's notion of creation as subtraction and addition, which is now oriented to human production, namely that design and invention are the father and mother of all and not merely one of the arts. However, that also creates a tension, and one of some significance in all later debates. He found that the ornamentation was muddled and imperfect, because in their columns they failed to observe correct measurements and proportions, nor did they distinguish the orders, and instead of being distinctly Doric, Corinthian, Ionic or Tuscan, 'they were confused and based on some anarchic rule'. Because the designs they invented were copies from antique remains or sprang from their own imagination, the building plans showed both the influence of sound architecture as well as contemporary improvisation, 'with the result that when the walls were raised the results were very different from the models'. It remains for Massacio to really accomplish the 'modern style'.

From Vasari we have lively and compelling anecdotes which throw light on the different ways models are used and considered, and something of the fate of models and the difficulty of their survival. We can trace the idea of the model as a means of communication and of securing a commission through his life of Lorenzo Ghiberti.

When Ghiberti was forced to leave Florence in 1400 because of the outbreak of the plague, he settled in the Romagna. There he decorated a room in Rimini for the art-loving young Prince Pandolfo Malatesta, who 'even as a young man took great pleasure in the art of design', and continued his studies, practising working in relief, stucco, wax, and concentrating on those small works which, Vasari adds, a sculptor knows as the preparatory sketches necessary to achieve perfection in the finished work.

Meanwhile in Florence the Signoria and the cloth-merchants guild discussed how a start should finally be made on the two doors of San Giovanni. They invited for competition specimens of a scene in bronze similar to those Andrea Pisano had made for the first door. For the seven artists finally chosen and voted a salary, it was stipulated that by the end of one year they should complete an example of the work in bronze of the same size as those in the first door. The scene chosen was Abraham sacrificing Isaac, because it was considered a test of their skills, since this required landscape, nude and draped figures and animals, and needed to show the important figures in full relief, the secondary figures in half relief and the tertiary in low relief.

Presented before 34 judges, the competitors Donatello and Brunelleschi, on seeing the scene made by Ghiberti and how carefully it was executed so that he 'seemed to have breathed into shape matter rather than cast it with polished iron tools', urged he be given the commission, for not to do so would be a shame for the city.

Much of Ghiberti's working life would be taken up with the doors, and Vasari is effulgent in his praise of the third door, 'the finest masterpiece ever created'. After all, he whom he admired was admired by him whom he most admired. Michelangelo had claimed that they were the doors of paradise: *O divinum opus*! Ghiberti in his own commentary would point to a similar conclusion, showing that the development of art culminated in his own work, with a display of erudition and vanity that had become mandatory for many artists at the period.

The model for the door which Vasari had seen as a young man in the Borgo Allegri, had been let go to ruin by Ghiberti's descendants. The juxtaposition perhaps holds a melancholy intimation of decline and fall: after all, it was in the Borgo Allegri that the citizens had gathered to see Cimabue's Our Lady painting for the Church of Santa Maria Novella, when it was visited by the old French King Charles of Anjou, and led to the area being indeed named the Joyful District on account of the event, 'Borgo Allegri'. The discarding of models has been their principal historical fate.

In commenting on the commission from the merchant's guild for a nine-foot-high statue of John the Baptist for one of the pilasters outside Orsanmichele, put into position in 1414, Vasari sees it as exhibiting the modern style, precisely in the degree of verisimilitude, in the heads and one of the arms 'that looks like living flesh'. Lorenzo, he notes, was the first to imitate the arts of the Ancient Romans which he studied very carefully 'as must everyone who wants to do good work'.[117]

Perhaps the most fascinating discussion of the artist and the model in this period is the story surrounding the congress held by the wardens of the works of Santa Maria del Fiore in the company of the consuls of the wool guild, which was called to assemble architects and engineers to discuss how to raise the cupola. It is the story of Brunelleschi 'who was sent from heaven to renew the art of architecture', and from whom the world received that great *maraviglia*, 'the greatest, the tallest, and the finest edifice of ancient and modern times'. The vertical, as this comment shows, was to become a new element for architecture and the idea of the physical wonder associated with the achievement of human invention.

The issue of invention and its relation to the creative process points to the new significance models would occupy in the period of Vasari's contemporaries, in that the realisation of the model becomes itself one of the significant parts of

117 Ibid., p.68.

[1]

[2]

[3]

Cristoforo Rocchi and Giovan Pietro
~~ga~~zza, Dome of Pavia, 16th century.
~~de~~tail.
Cristoforo Rocchi and Giovan Pietro
~~Ga~~zza, Dome of Pavia, 16th century.
~~A~~ntonio da Sangallo, model of the project
~~for~~ the St Peter's Basilica, Rome,
~~15~~39-1546.

the realisation of large projects and buildings. The model not only is a referee within the different developments of the project, but importantly a direct means of communication and persuasion to a non-specialist public; it therefore acts as a critical instrument between practitioners and an interested public. In spite of the fact that we have only a small fraction of surviving models, their significance both for the crystallisation of the architectural idea, as a means of communication to patrons and clients and the public, and their place when built in workshops can be adduced. For example, some of the models were of large dimension and, placed in workshops, acted as a normative regulation of representation and a direct instrument of control.

The tension which can be expressed in the model as a generator of the architectural idea and the requirement of communication also points to constraints for the working method. The story Vasari offers of Brunelleschi is highly instructive, and gathers up many of the features which have already been outlined. It bears close scrutiny. The story of Vasari begins by pointing not to the corpus architectura, but directly to the physical appearance of the architect; that is, the architect's body, which in the instance of Filippo Brunelleschi is regarded as unprepossessing, with Vasari having us understand that he was small and insignificant but fiercely consumed by ambition and eager to tackle difficulty. The fine grace and bearing with which nature should endow the artist is missing in this case, as it was, Vasari suggests, with Giotto. That the small and insignificant architect's body should build the tallest and most elegant building in the world is almost forwarded by Vasari as a strange conceit, a paradox that does not flow from the order of nature, and again one can see how throughout the lives the early reference to the divine in creation is being inevitably handed to the human as possessed of divine possibility. This is a reverse incarnation. Further, it instates clearly the fundamental difference between the creator and creatures along another disjunction, that of nature and the human, since human making is of another process and purpose than that which is issued by nature itself, in which the notion of production is not relevant.

There is a further tension, one that Alberti fails to fully explicate. The divine order in its perfection does not as macrocosmos entail that the microcosmos of man in his making has no room for anything other than the mimesis of the perfect order. This would be to deprive creatures of freedom. The searching and process in making at the human level has its own order, and is no longer simply a domain of grace, but of work, trial and error, production, and the hard and often strenuous achievement of mortality. If the divine order incarnates itself necessarily to include the finite, then human making achieves divinity precisely in the reach of its finite struggles.

Vasari supplies a curiously compensatory genealogy, stressing the learning and distinguished background of Filippo, and again a reversal takes place. The boy is too intelligent to learn at school, his detachment suggesting he was preoccupied with things others than the rudiments of reading and writing. He is, against the father's wish that he should be an attorney like his grandfather, apprenticed to the goldsmith's art with a friend of his, 'so that he might learn design'. He occupied himself with engraving on silver, and silver figures, and made figures in bas-relief, indicating future possibilities. Through discussion with learned friends, he became interested in time and motion, and weights and wheels, and this resulted in his making some very 'beautiful clocks'.

Thanks to his friendship with Donatello he practised making sculpture. But his talent as an architect showed itself because of his work on houses, that of his relation Apolloni Lapi at the corner of the Ciai, towards the Old Market, and of course in the Palazzo della Signoria, where he arranged all those rooms where the Monte met to transact their business, 'constructing doors and window in a style which had been employed in the ancient world but was also then out of fashion because of the crudeness of contemporary architecture'. The latter comment indicates the 'barbarous German style that was then fashionable'. With Donatello he travelled to Rome. He had sold his farm in Settignano and they studied and measured with amazement the Roman monuments, Vasari adding that Brunelleschi studied so intensely he often didn't sleep or eat. There he harboured also the secret ambition, which he did not even confide to Donatello, of solving the problem of raising the cupola at Santa Maria dell Fiore. In Rome he 'continually investigated all the problems that had been involved in vaulting the Pantheon'.[118] Their studies continued even in the face of local suspicion that they were treasure-hunters or practising necromancy.

Brunelleschi now masters the *corpus architectura*, there being no kind of building of which he did not make drawings; round, square, and octagonal temples, basilicas, aqueducts, baths, arches, colosseums, amphitheatres, and all the brick temples from which he noted the methods used in binding and clamping with ties and encircling the vaults. He learned to distinguish the several orders, and his studies were so intelligent and thorough that, 'in his mind's eye he could see Rome as it stood before it fell into ruins'. Vasari is clearly setting out a programme of studies in this paratactic list, in which curiosity and intelligence restore the power of the imagination to visualise and picture a past.

Returning from Rome to Florence in 1407, he participated in the conference called to tackle the raising of the cupola. He directly suggested that Arnolfo's plans should be disregarded, and instead that a frieze thirty feet high should be constructed, with a large round window in each of its sides, since this would take the weight off the supports of the tribunes and also make it easier to raise the cupola. 'Following this models were designed and executed',[119] and 'Filippo stayed in Florence many months, quietly making models and machines for the cupola, talking and joking every day with the other craftsmen'. During this time he even went along to help Ghiberti with the polishing of the doors.

118 Ibid., p.140.
119 Ibid., p.141.

[1]

[2]

1 Antonio da Sangallo, model of the proje[ct]
for the St Peter's Basilica, Rome, 1539-
1546.
2 Ventura Vittoni [?], Chiesa di Santa Ma[ria]
dell Consolazione, Todi, 1597-1598.

Filippo then showed that his affability and joviality was also married to immense shrewdness. He left for Rome, guessing correctly that the confident outline he had given of a solution could not proceed without him, and he awaited his recall to Florence which duly took place. This allowed him deliver an artful and finely ambivalent speech to the wardens of Santa Maria del Fiore and the consuls of the wool guild, in which he laid out that great projects present great problems. He had thought about the project but could never make up his mind. It was more daunting than the Partheon in Rome. Unlike the Partheon, they would have to use another method, following the eight sides using ties and dovetailing the stones. Anyway, he had not yet thought of the solution, but they could go ahead and gather architects from all over and then come up with something, and of course a Church dedicated to God and the Virgin could expect some divine inspiration or help.

They urged him to make a model. Again he refused, they offered money, pleaded, but, instead he left for Rome, where he spent all his time studying how to vault the cupola. He had talked himself into a corner, and now a supreme achievement would be required. By 1420, architects were assembled, and Filippo attended the meeting. This meeting turned into a fiasco, with Filippo's suggestion being dubbed insane. In a sense he may have deliberately risked this, as Vasari reports that he could have shown them a small model he had made for the project but was reluctant to do so because of lack of understanding among the consuls, the jealousy of other artists and the fickleness of the crowds.

The meeting, which finally gave Filippo the commission, was again the result of intense lobbying on his part, and eventuated in a piece of one-upmanship bordering on the farcical. He was asked again to show his plans and models, and instead he rejoined whoever could make an egg stand on a flat piece of marble should build the cupola. They all failed; he took the egg, cracked it at the bottom and placed it standing on the marble. This allowed him to also tell why he wouldn't show the model or plans. He was awarded the commission. It was thirteen years since he had returned to the first meeting in Florence to discuss the raising of the cupola. The project was given to Filippo, but again another convolution and intrigue required he share the superintendence with Ghiberti.

In the meantime Filippo conceived the ambition to make a model surpassing anything done previously; he set his hand to making the design, and then he had it executed by a carpenter named Bartolommeo, who lived near the studio. In this model, which was exactly to scale, he made all the difficult structures, such as the lighted and the dark stairways, and all kinds of round windows, ties and buttresses, as well as part of the gallery. Ghiberti was not allowed see the model, and set to make his own. Whereas Filippo was paid fifty lire and fifteen soldi for his model, which figure Vasari takes from the account book of Migliori di Tomasso, October 3rd 1419, Ghiberti was paid 300 lire for the work on his model.

Filippo bided his time. Ghiberti or friends were trying increasingly to take credit for the design. When the vault was at 24 feet, and the difficult operation of placing the wooden and stone ties had to be undertaken, Filippo, in a drama of buffo proportions, took to his bed with a bandaged head, and left the masons and builders to deal with Ghiberti, who not having seen the model and not knowing Filippo's mind had to hedge his bets in all answers as to how to proceed.

The taking a-bed of Filippo was interpreted as remorse at ever having undertaken the project. It was a calculated coup de théatre to put Ghiberti on the spot and force him from the project. The final demasking of Ghiberti was that Filippo insisted they share the work equally. There were two main problems remaining, one the scaffolding and the other binding the ties. Ghiberti chose the binding, as he thought the earlier vault construction of Brunelleschi would give him the necessary directions.

Meanwhile Ghiberti had only completed the ties on one of the eight sides and Filippo let it be known he did not think it would suffice for the loadbearing requirement from the pressure of the vault. It was then that Filippo delivered the coup de grâce; he, on command, produced his models and designs. This was to lead to a dramatic reversal, with Filippo receiving large cash payments and complete control over the supervision, which he would exercise with a fanatical heart over some years. Ghiberti's contract had not terminated, and would run for three more years, and the making of models became a mischief in which Brunelleschi was harried by supporters of Ghiberti and artists and citizens who involved themselves in the case of the construction:

> Filippo, meanwhile, was always, on the slightest excuse, making designs and models for scaffolds for the builders and of machines for lifting weights. But this did not prevent some malicious people (who were friends of Lorenzo) from throwing him into despair by continuously having other models constructed in competition with his; some, which were made by Antonio da Verzelli and other favoured artists, were put forward for attention now by one citizen and now by another, in a way showing how fickle they were, for they knew little and understood less, and how although they had perfect work within their reach they were ready to promote imperfect and worthless things.[120]

A stand-off by the masons for higher pay was to result in 'scab labour' being introduced, and the masons and workers forced to accept less. They had tried to gang up against the omnipresent overseer to find that they had to return and work for lower pay.

Vasari then informs us that the tide turned in Filippo's favour, and that those who were not already prejudiced maintained that he had demonstrated a boldness such that no other ancient or modern architect had ever shown:

This was because he brought out his model for the cupola and let everyone see the tremendous thought he had given to the planning of the stairways: there were lights both inside and out (so that no-one might be frightened and injured in the darkness) and several iron guiderails placed where the ascent was steep. Everything was very carefully arranged. As well as this, he had thought of irons for fixing scaffolding inside, in case there was a need to do mosaics or painting; he also placed the different kinds of gutter, some covered and some open, in the least dangerous positions; and along with these he designed various holes and apertures to break the force of the wind and prevent exhalations or movements of the earth from causing any damage.[121]

All of this indicated to Vasari how much he had profited from his years of study in Rome.

The attention to detail is well captured in the fact that he would take time to visit the kilns where the bricks were being baked, and would insists on seeing and handling the clay, and selecting them carefully with his own hands. He also inspected the stone to see if they were hard and unflawed, 'and he would give them models for the joints and turning made of wood or wax, or cut from a turnip', and similarly he made iron tools for the smiths.[122]

When the time came to start closing the vaults towards the round window where the lantern was to be erected, he again produced different models he had made in Rome and Florence. These again had not been shown before to anyone. 'Filippo also made with his own hand a model for the lantern'. Again Vasari details the lively and complex scene, when another skirmish in the battle of the models started up. In the model for the lantern, Filippo had covered his tracks with a blocking up of the entrance which he alone knew. Nevertheless the model mania was not to be discouraged and various artists in Florence began making models of their own. Vasari reports: 'a woman of the Gaddi family was bold enough to enter one in competition with Filippo's.' The situation became so odd in some way that friends of Brunelleschi advised him not to show his own model, but this he brushed off with the comment: 'there was only one good model and the others were worthless'. When he saw some of the ways in which artists had 'borrowed' from his model, he quipped: 'The next model this man makes will be mine'.

In another moment of poker playing with the wardens, he finally took away the block to seeing where the ascent led to the ball. He revealed also the little piece of wood in a pilaster leading to the staircase as it is seen today. Being old, he stipulated how it should be built after his death, leaving a model and written instructions.

The most famous model of the period and the one of which Vasari gives the most detailed account is that of Michelangelo for the drum and dome of St. Peter's. This commission, which was one of the most important in the Renaissance, was eagerly sought by Michelangelo. There are two paintings showing Michelangelo presenting models, one of the model of San Lorenzo,

120 Ibid., p.155.
121 Ibid., pp.156-157.
122 Ibid., p.157.

the subject of a painting commissioned from Da Empoli (1554-1640). The painting is now housed at the Casa Buonarroti in Florence, and shows Michelangelo presenting the model to Pope Leo x and the Cardinal Guiliano de Medici, later Pope Clement, in the company of members of the Curia and courtiers. Lying on the table is also unfurled the plan for the Laurentian library and one can see the stairs in plan about which Michelangelo has sent a charming and detailed account by letter to Vasari, quoted in the Lives. That letter also throws considerable light on his working method and what can be called creative if serendipitous model making:

> Giorgio, my dear friend, Concerning the stairway for the library that I've been asked about so much, believe me if I could remember how I planned it I would not need to be asked. A certain staircase comes to my mind, just like a dream, though I don't think it can be the same as the one I had in mind originally, since it seems so awkward … However, I'll describe it for you, it is as if you took a number of oval boxes, each one a span deep, but not of the same length or width, and placed the largest down on the paving further from or nearer to the wall with the door, depending on the gradient wanted for the stairs. Then it is as if you place another box on top of the first, smaller than the first and leaving all round enough space for the foot to ascend, and so on, diminishing and drawing back the steps towards the door, always with enough space to climb, and the last step should be the same size as the opening of the door … and this oval stairway should have two wings … one on either side, following the centre steps but straight instead of oval … The ends of the two wings should face the walls and, with the entire staircase, come about three spans from the wall, leaving the lower part of each wall of the anteroom completely unobstructed. I am writing nonsense, but I know you will find something here to your purpose.[123]

The second is the painting by Domenico Cresti Da Passignano (1558/60-1636). The artist is shown pointing to the model, as is the Pope, and the gesture of Michelangelo's hand wittily echoes the crumpled finger and loose wrist of Adam from the Sistine Chapel, that of the Pope the hand of God. In this instance it is 'Adam' who is the creator. What is being pointed to is a model whose scale we can grasp from the fact that it is almost occluded from view by the courtier in the left of the picture, and is therefore, as an object, thought to be on a human

123 Ibid., pp.400-401.

Painting of the Pope looking at the model, and plans of the San Lorenzo, library and stairs.

The cupola of the Basilica of St Peter's, Rome.

scale, even though as we can see the presentation in the picture alters the actual scale and aspects of the model which point away from the original as conceived by Michelangelo. The most detailed account was provided in the Washington Gallery show of 1988 and the catalogue published that same year.[124]

Setting the depiction of Da Empoli against the account of Vasari suggests strongly that the model as chosen in the painting has the alterations of Da Porta made shortly after the death of Michelangelo. In one sense one can say that the alterations strip the model of Florentine and specifically Brunelleschian features which were maintained by Michelangelo. Michelangelo built most of the drum of the dome, and certainly invented the projecting radial spurs that provide such a dynamic alternation of relief and depth as they ascend upward to the ribs of the dome. The dome was built twenty years after Michelangelo's death in 1564. With regard to the model of the drum and dome, the Washington concluded that it was not in its original state, and the current survivor, which was restored to Michelangelo's design by Ackerman's researches, incorporates changes made by Giacomo Della Porta, who worked on the dome after the death of Michelangelo, and the mid-18th century architect Vanvitelli, who was consulted about the stability of the structure and whose drawings indicated the state of the drum and dome as shown. There are also surviving drawings from Michelangelo and assistants that indicate how Michelangelo developed his design, and these can be supplemented by the drawings of Giovanni Antonio Dosio, which reveal developmental stages in the design during the construction of the model of the drum and dome. The best representation is considered to be the drawings from the shop of the French architect Etienne Duperac, made in preparation for sets of prints which were published. All of this various evidence needs to be set against the detailed account of Vasari. The description can very well have been written whilst the model was being constructed, with details indicated which were later changed in the final design.

What is known is that Michelangelo completed in terracotta a model of the drum and dome in July 1557, datable to five years after he completed the base of the dome and after the beginning of the construction of the drum. Construction had been interrupted in 1566 just as the drum was reaching the height of the window cills. It may be that it was also becoming clear that Michelangelo, now 81 years of age, was ready to accept the invitation of Duke Cosimo and leave Rome for good. Indeed Vasari's evidence is that even his best friends, the Cardinal of Carpi and Tommaso de Cavalieri, urged him to supply a model.

The terracotta model was finished in July 1557, but work on the wood model did not go forward until November 1558. It was finished in November 1561, exactly three years later. It is possible to see from dated records to cabinetmakers, listed by Millon and Smyth, payments made for capitals from April to November 1559, for columns in the summer of 1560, for the balusters on the interior cornice in November 1560, from September to May 1561 for heavy paper to make an

124 H. Millon, **Michelangelo Architect** (Olivetti, 1988).

initial model of the lantern, and for wood members of the final lantern in the autumn of 1561. The payments recorded for the small and large tondi of the interior dome were also made during this time. Vasari's description and one of the drawings of Dosio include ovals as the decorative elements of the interior dome, and not tondi. Further, their descriptions and drawings do not agree about the lantern. Neither record the final design.

It is possible to turn to Vasari's account, which then provides a snapshot of the work in progress on the model. Another vital piece of evidence is that the drawing of Dosio shows the resumption of work six months after the model was completed, indicating the drum was under construction in the last year of Michelangelo's life. By the time of his death in February 1564 the drum had reached the height of the capitals of the column buttresses, and most of the capitals were in place.

The continuation of the work by Pirro Ligorio and Vignola was suspended in 1568, and the entablature was left incomplete. These were only finished in 1588 by Giacomo Della Porta, and between 1588 and 1593 he built the attic of the drum, the inner and outer domes, and the lantern above. The profile of the drum, as Millon and Smyth note, is elevated and not hemispherical. The drawings of Duperac confirmed for these scholars the question that had also been tackled by Wittkower and conclude that both domes of the model in its original state were hemispherical. Michelangelo will have remembered Brunelleschi's dome in Florence and also Brunelleschi's studious obsession with the dome of the Pantheon.

Surviving sources indicate that Michelangelo made small clay models, which must be taken as a means of studying three-dimensional effects. The first try in terracotta in response to the imploring of friends allowed such a study through the modelling of the clay. Ackerman has made the point that Michelangelo preferred clay models to perspective sketches, as he thought of the building as experiences in movement, and the model also allowed the study of the three-dimensionality of the object.

Turning to Vasari, one can see that the situation of a lull in construction had made the friends of Michelangelo anxious (Cardinal di Carpi, Francesco Bandini, Lottino and Tommaso de Cavalieri). Michelangelo is described as being much pressed and even constrained by them to make a model. He procrastinated. Months elapsed before he could resolve what to do. He then hesitantly made a beginning, and produced a small model in clay, 'un piccolo modello di terra', and with the aid of plans and sections which he also prepared, 'there might eventually be a much larger one in wood'. Vasari says that such a model was made in less than a year by Maestro Giovanni Franzese, and that the dimensions and minute proportions of this smaller structure measured by the Roman palm corresponded in every particular with those of the cupola.

Vasari goes on to say that all the parts of the model were executed with

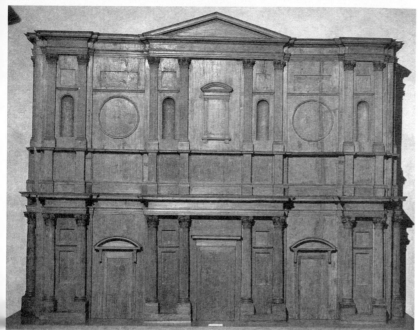

[1]

[2]

Michelangelo, Church of San Lorenzo.
açade.
Michelangelo, Church of San Lorenzo.
etail of model façade.

[1]

[2]

[3]

1, 2, 3 A comparison of domes: the dome of
St Peter's [Michelangelo], the dome of
Florence [Brunelleschi], and the dome of the
Pantheon [Piranesi].

extreme nicety, the members of the columns, the bases, the capitals, doors, windows, cornices, ressauts, and every other detail, by Michelangelo in the best way.

Vasari then suggests crucially that he has written about objects of much less importance and is undertaking to give an account of the design according to which Michelangelo proposed to construct the church and cupola. Rather than just the rhetorical use of eckphrasis, Vasari's minute descriptions in his writings are there to safeguard the intentions of Michelangelo, should he not live to see the project to completion: 'so my writing will help to assist the faithful execution of the designs, and restrain the malignity of those presuming persons who may desire to alter them'. Despite writing one of the most detailed descriptions every given of an architectural model, Vasari's wish was not fulfilled, and ultimately neither that of the artist who above all others in history, for Vasari, not excluding the ancients, could be called in his power of creation, divine.

Selected References

Agrest, Diana, **Architecture from Without. Theoretical Framings for a Critical Practice** (MIT Press, 1991).

Alberti, **De Re Aedificatoria**,1485 (New York: Dover, 1986).

Bachelard, Gaston, **Le matérialisme rationnel** (Paris: PUF, 1953).

Barasch, Moshe, **Theories of Art from Plato to Winckleman** (New York University Press, 1985).

Baudrillard, Jean, **Simulacra and Simulation** (Ann Arbor: The University of Michigan Press, 1994).

Beckmann, John (ed.), **The Virtual Dimension: Architecture Representation and Crash Culture** (New York: Princeton Architectural Press, 1998).

Benedetti, Sandro, 'The Model of Saint Peter's', **The Renaissance from Brunelleschi to Michelangelo**, ed. H.A. Millon (London: Thames and Hudson, 1996).

Benevolo, Leonard, **History of Modern Architecture** (MIT Press, 1977).

Black, Max, **Models and Metaphors** (Ithaca: Cornell University Press, 1962).

Bohm, David, **Causality and Chance in Modern Physics** (London: Routledge, 1976).

Bohr, Niels, **Atomic Theory and the Description of Nature** (New York: Macmillan, 1934).

Bradley, J., **Mach's Philosophy of Science** (London: Athlone Press, 1971).

Braithwaite, R.B., 'Models in the Empirical Sciences', **Logic, Methodology and the Philosophy of Science**, eds. Nagel, Suppes, Tarski (Stanford, California, 1962).

Broglie, Louis de, **La physique nouvelle et les quanta** (Paris: Flammarion, 1937).

Brown, J.R., **The Laboratory of the Mind: Thought Experiments in the Natural Sciences** (London: Routledge, 1991).

Cable, Carole, **The Architectural Model** (Vance Bibliographies, 1982).

Carnap, Rudolph, **Scheinsprobleme in der Philosophie** (Hamburg: Felix Meiner, 1928).

Carpo, Mario, **Architecture in the Age of Printing**, trans. Sarah Benson (MIT Press, 2001).
'How Do You Imitate a Building that You Have Never Seen? Printed Images, Ancient Models, and Handmade Drawings in Renaissance Architectural Theory', in **Zeitschrift fur Kunstgeschichte**, 64 (2001), pp.223-233.
La Maschera e il Modello (Milan: Jaca Book, 1993).

Choay, Francoise, **The Rule and the Model: On the Theory of Architecture and Urbanism** (MIT Press, 1997).

Crick, Francis, 'The genetic code', in **Scientific American**, October 1962, pp.66-74.

Deleuze, Gilles, **Spinoza et le problème de l'expression** (Paris: Editions de Minuit, 1968).
Logique du sens (Paris: PUF, 1969).

De l'Orme, Philibert, **Le premier tome de l'architecture** (Paris: Federic Morel, 1567).

Dijksterhuis, E.J., **De Mechanisering van het Wereldbeeld** (Amsterdam: Meulenhoff, 1950).

Dinsmoor, William, 'The Literary Remains of Sebastiano Serlio', in **The Art Bulletin**, XXIV (1942), pp.59-91,115-15.

Duhem, Pierre, **The Aim and Structure of Physical Theory** (Princeton: Princeton University Press, 1954).

Eliade, Mircea, **The Sacred and Profane** (Holt Rinehart and Wilson, 1963).

Filarete, Antonio, **Trattato de architettura**, ed. Anna Finoli and Liliana Grassi (Milan: Il Polifilo, 1972).

Foucault, Michel, **Les Mots et les Choses** (Paris: Gallimard, 1966).

Frampton, Kenneth, **Silvia Kolbowski, Idea as Model**, catalogue 3, Institute for Architecture and Urban Studies (Rizzoli International Publications, 1983).

Frascari, Marco, **Monsters of Architecture** (Rowman and Littlefield, 1991).

Frey, G., **Symbolische und Ikonische Modelle** (Synthese, September 1960), pp.213-221.

Galison, Peter, **How Experiments End** (Chicago: University of Chicago Press, 1987).

Giedion, Sigfried, **Mechanization Takes Command** (New York: Oxford University Press, 1948).

Gombrich, Ernst, **The Sense of Order** (Cornell University Press, 1975).

Goodman, Nelson, **Fact, Fiction and Forecast** (Harvard University Press, 1983).

Granger, Frank, **Vitruvius on Architecture** (Harvard University Press, 1983).

Hacking, Ian, **Representing and Intervening** (Cambridge: Cambridge University Press, 1983).
Scientific Revolutions (Oxford: Oxford University Press, 1981).

Haldane, J.B.S., **On Being the Right Size and Other Essays**, ed. John M. Smith (Oxford: Oxford University Press, 1985).

Harmon, Robert, **Architectural Models** (Vance Bibliographies, 1980).

Hersey, George, **The Lost Meaning of Classical Architecture** (MIT Press, 1988).

Hitchcock, Henry-Russell and Philip Johnson, **The International Style (1932)** (Norton, 1995).

Hoenen, P., **Cosmologia** (Rome: Gregorian University, 1956).

Hutten, E.H., 'The role of models in physics', in **British Journal of the Philosophy of Science**, 4, no.16, 1954, pp.284-301.

Janke, Rolf, **Architectural Models** (London: Thames and Hudson, 1968).

Joost-Gaugier, Christiane L., **Measuring Heaven** (Ithaca and London: Cornell University Press, 2006).

Kahn, Louis, **Between Silence and Light** (New York: Random House, 1979).

Kearney, Richard, **The Wake of the Imagination** (University of Minnesota Press, 1988).

King, Ross, **Brunelleschi's Dome** (London: Chatto and Windus, 2000).

Koyré, Alexandre, **From the Closed World to the Infinite Universe** (Baltimore: Johns Hopkins, 1957).

Kuhn, Thomas S., **The Structure of Scientific Revolutions** (Chicago: University of Chicago Press, 1962).

Kurrent, Friedrich (ed.), **Scale Models: Houses of the 20th Century** (Basle: Birkhäuser Verlag, 1999).

Lehmann, Karl, 'The Dome of Heaven', **Art Bulletin**, XXVI, 1945, pp.1-27.

Leroi-Gourhan, André, **Milieu et techniques** (Paris: Albin Michel, 1943-45).

Lucci, Robert, **Design Models** (Van Nostrand Reinhold, 1989).

Millon, Henry (ed.), **Italian Renaissance Architecture from Brunelleschi to Michelangelo** (London: Thames and Hudson, 1996).
The Triumph of the Baroque Architecture in Europe, 1600-1750 (London: Thames and Hudson, 1999).
'Observations on a newly discovered wood model for the south hemicycle vault of Michelangelo's St. Peter's', in **Journal of the Society of Architectural Historians**, XXIX, 1970, p.265.

'Models in Renaissance Architecture', **The Renaissance from Brunelleschi to Michelangelo** (London: Thames and Hudson, 1996).

Morris, Mark, **Models: Architecture and the Miniature** (London: Wiley, 2006).

Nauta, Doede, **Logica en Model** (Hilversum: De Haan, 1969).

Neumann, Dietrich, **Film Architecture: From Metropolis to Blade Runner** (Munich: Prestel, 1999).

Onians, John, **Bearers of Meaning** (Princeton: Princeton University Press, 1988).

Philandrier, Guillaume, **In Decem libros M. Vitruvii Pollionis Annotationes** (Rome, 1544).

Porter, Tom and John Neale, **Architectural Supermodels** (Oxford: Architectural Press, 2000).

Puppi, Lionello, 'Modelli di Palladio, modelli palladiani', in **Rassegna**, 9, 32, 1987.

Rykwert, Joseph, **The Necessity of Artifice** (Rizzoli International Publication, 1982).

Serlio, Sebastiano, **Regole generali di architettura** (Venice, 1537).

Smith, Albert C., **Architectural Model as Machine** (London: Elsevier, 2004).

Tafuri, Manfredo, **The Sphere and the Labyrinth** (MIT Press, 1987).

Vitruvio, **Nella cultura architettonica antica medievale e moderna, a cura di Gianluigi Ciotta** (Genova, 2001).

Acknowledgements

It is a pleasure to acknowledge the help I have had in the preparation of this publication. In the first place my best thanks to Professor Arie Graafland, who as the Director of the Delft School of Design at the Faculty of Architecture, Delft University of Technology, has given unstinted support to this project since its inception.

The Delft School of Design has been also a shelter for diverse research interests. In earlier publications, **The Body in Architecture**, **Crossover**, and **De-/signing the Urban**, edited by Deborah Hauptmann, Leslie Kavanaugh and Gerhard Bruyns respectively, one can see how the various strands of doctoral research, conference papers and design topics have been gathered, and how this has granted a view to all participants over the last five years into the range and extent of practice in design and architectural theory current in the international community, and also afforded an insight into the complex cross-currents of debates and positions in architecture.

This publication is the fourth in a series from the DSD, and has taken up for discussion material germane to the earlier works, namely the relationship of arguments about the process of design in the body-mind-machine triplex, which has been such a determinant of architectural discourse since the work of Vitruvius.

I also remember with great pleasure the visit to the DSD of and lively discussion with Karsten Harries. Professor Harries is one among the many distinguished guests who have visited and participated at the DSD, among whom Michael Hays, Edward Soja, Stan Allen, Michael Speaks, Christine Boyer, Anthony Vidler, Joan Busquets and Scott Lash.

I have benefited immensely from association with this forum and especially from weekly seminars over a period of four years. To the participants at these seminars I would like to express my deepest thanks, among whom Stephen Read, Deborah Hauptmann, Alexander Vollebregt, Gerhard Bruyns, Augustina Martire, Camilo Pinilla, Jeroen van Schaick, Qiang Sheng, Alta Steenkamp, Lara Schrijver, Axel Çoruh, Gregory Bracken, Isabelle Doucet, Akkelies van Nes, Brent Bastra, Heidi Sohn and Ceren Sezer. In some cases participants have contributed unpublished research papers and in many cases detailed discussions, for which I am most grateful. Some of their recent work can be followed in numbers 1 and 2 of the new journal of the Delft School of Design, **Footprint**, which is available electronically.

In the Model Department of the Faculty of Architecture I have also had the benefit of discussion with Jack Breen, Martijn Stellingwerff and others. They kindly supplied me with copies of publications and made me aware of their discussion on the virtual context of design, model making and the significance of the model as a means of communication, which I have emphasised in my reading of Alberti's theoretical account.

I would like to also thank Christoph Grafe and Professor Tony Fretton for often fleeting but instructive conversations.

Naturally I should like to thank the students at the Faculty. Who, standing under the entrance baldachino, can forget the sight of students, often cycling against strong crosswinds from the West, and their difficult act of balancing as many came to the Faculty with models, often precariously wrapped, and nevertheless contrived to arrive without falling? Nothing could remind one more of the fragility of models, and the difficulty of their survival, a point often reiterated by Vasari, than this frequent sight at the Faculty door.

I am therefore especially happy that literally days before the terrible fire which destroyed the Faculty building in May of this year, Gerhard Bruyns had the idea of photographing models **in situ** in the physical plant, and thus a collective record of much student work displayed along the fourth floor of the Department of Interiors, has been illustrated in this publication. I would also like to thank him for his assistance on the final shape of the publication, which has been so invaluable and has involved him in long hours of research.

To the Dean of the Faculty, who in the days following the fire mustered the entire community and enabled everyone to continue as best as possible with their work, no thank-you is sufficient. Graduation projects and other research commitments have continued largely uninterrupted and the hospitality of the University to a suddenly homeless group of scholars was and continues to be, indeed, exemplary.

The publishing house of 010 Rotterdam also deserve the best thanks possible, for their assistance by all manner and means in the production of this work, which has been prepared in time for presentation at the Venice Biennale, at the Dutch Pavilion, to the director of the NAi Rotterdam, an honour of which I am very mindful. Of course I must say that without the stalwart work of John Kirkpatrick this publication would not have made it intact to the printer.

In Amsterdam I would like very much to thank Gijs van Koningsveld for all his work on the text in an earlier stage, whose copy-editing and close reading was of enormous help. I would like also to thank his father Professor van Koningsveld for kindly looking over the Arabic transcriptions and making helpful suggestions.

There are other individuals whom I should like to name for support and discussion, among whom Johannes Schwarz, Brendan O'Byrne, Daniel Caffrey, Oran Hoffmann, Frank Callanan and Taf Hassam. To each and every one my thanks, and this with the mitigating plea that I alone am responsible for views and opinions expressed in this extended essay on the model and its architecture.

Patrick Healy, Amsterdam, July 13th 2008.

Credits

Delft School of Design Series on Architecture and Urbanism
Series Editor Arie Graafland

Editorial Board
K. Michael Hays (Harvard University, USA)
Ákos Moravánszky (ETH Zürich, Switzerland)
Michael Müller (Bremen University, Germany)
Frank R. Werner (University of Wuppertal, Germany)
Gerd Zimmermann (Bauhaus University, Germany)

Also published in this series:
1 **Crossover. Architecture Urbanism Technology**
ISBN 978 90 6450 609 3
2 **The Body in Architecture**
ISBN 978 90 6450 568 3
3 **De-/signing the Urban. Technogenesis and the urban image**
ISBN 978 90 6450 611 6

The Model and its Architecture
Author Patrick Healy
Text editing Gijs van Koningsveld, John Kirkpatrick
Book design by Piet Gerards Ontwerpers (Piet Gerards and
Maud van Rossum), Amsterdam
Printed by DeckersSnoeck, Antwerp

Photo credits Gerhard Bruyns, cover

©2008 The author / 010 Publishers, Rotterdam
www.010.nl

ISBN 978 90 6450 684 0